**W9-CNA-298**

# The
# ASTROLOGY of
# TRANSFORMATION

# The ASTROLOGY of TRANSFORMATION

## A Multilevel Approach by

# Dane Rudhyar

This publication made possible with
the assistance of the Kern Foundation

**The Theosophical Publishing House**
**Wheaton, Ill. U.S.A.**
**Madras, India/London, England**

Library of Congress Cataloging in Publication Data

Rudhyar, Dane
   The astrology of transformation
   1. Astrology.      I. Title.
BF1708.1.R836      133.5      80-51553
ISBN 0-8356-0542-6
Printed in the United States of America

Cover art from *Jewel of the Essence of all Science,* Treatise 1840, India

To Leyla
  Whose sustainment and understanding
  enabled me to complete this book.
    With love,
      D.R.

# TABLE OF CONTENTS

PROLOGUE ................................. ix

1. THE TWO BASIC WAYS OF MEETING LIFE'S
   CONFRONTATIONS ...........................1
   The Yang Way................................4
   The Yin Way................................10

2. THE TWO FACES OF ASTROLOGY.............24
   An Astrology of Information....................28
   An Astrology of Understanding and Meaning......34

3. FOUR LEVELS OF INTERPRETING HUMAN
   EXPERIENCE AND ASTROLOGICAL DATA.....46
   Four Levels of Human Functioning..............46
   A Multilevel Astrology.........................51
   The Biological Level of Interpretation...........55
   The Sociocultural Level and the 'Person'..........60
   The Planets' Meanings at the Sociocultural Level...63
   Nodes, Eclipses and the Trans-Saturnian Planets...69

4. THE INDIVIDUAL LEVEL
   OF INTERPRETATION.......................75
   The Mandala Symbol in Astrology................75
   The Birth-Chart and the Planets in a
       Mandala-Type of Interpretation................85
   Going Beyond the Individual Level..............94

5. THE MARRIAGE OF MIND AND SOUL..........99

6. THE PRACTICE OF ASTROLOGY AT THE
   TRANSPERSONAL LEVEL.................... 115
   The Client's Readiness and the
      Astrologer's Responsibility..................119
   The Birth-Chart as a Symbol of Individual Karma.. 126
   The Transmutation of Karma into Dharma....... 131

7. INTERPRETING THE BIRTH-CHART AT THE
   TRANSPERSONAL LEVEL.................... 136
   A Transpersonal Interpretation of Sun,
      Moon and Planets..........................138
   Planetary Interactions: Aspects and Gestalt....... 149
   Angles: Root-factors in Personality and
      their Transformation........................156

8. PROGRESSIONS AND TRANSITS............. 163
   Personality as an Unfolding Process............. 163
   Secondary or 'Solar' Progressions............... 166
   Progressed Lunation Cycle: Progressed-to-natal vs.
      Progressed-to-Progressed Considerations.......173
   The Transits of the Planets.................... 180

   EPILOGUE ............................... 192

   INDEX...................................201

# PROLOGUE

This book could be called my astrological testament, in the sense that it brings to a conclusion my attempt to reformulate and give a new direction to modern astrology.

The first part of this 45-year-long endeavor began in 1933 when I started to write for the then new magazine *American Astrology*, founded by Paul Clancy, a series of monthly articles which was to last for more than twenty years. The first group of articles was used as a foundation for my book *,The Astrology of Personality*, published in 1936 at the request of Alice Bailey who had started the Lucis Press in New York.

This first part of my astrological work was brought to a conclusion in 1968 when I formed the International Committee for a Humanistic Astrology (ICHA) and wrote six essays now published as *Person-Centered Astrology* (N.Y.: A.S.I. Publishers). The second part began with the publication of *From Humanistic to Transpersonal Astrology* (Palo Alto, CA: Seed Center, 1975) and *The Sun Also a Star: The Galactic Dimension of Astrology* (N.Y.: A.S.I. Publishers). This present volume concludes what I am able to say concerning what I call 'transpersonal astrology.'

I began to use the term *transpersonal* in 1930, long before the movement of transpersonal psychology was started, and with a meaning quite different from the one the word has recently taken on in the field of psychology. I defined as transpersonal a process of 'descent' of transcendent spiritual power and illumination *through* the normal consciousness, and eventually through the whole personality of a human being. The source of that power and light exists in a realm 'beyond' the personal consciousness and the ego, but I saw in the transpersonal action a *descent* of power rather than an *ascent* of a person's consciousness and emotions. In traditional religious terms, as a man prays to God his soul reaches up to the Divine; and God answers by an outpouring of 'grace'—a descent of the Holy Spirit. The transpersonal approach I have been presenting does not follow any strictly religious system of thought; neither is it 'mystical' in the usual sense of the term. It is essentially metaphysical and cosmological—or one may say *cosmontological*, as it refers to cosmic 'being' *(ontos)*.

The term metaphysical, however, need not frighten anyone, because as I am using it, it simply refers to the expansion and generalization of very concrete, universal experiences and everyday modes of operation. For example, the two basic approaches to life-situations and personal problems I discuss in the first chapter of this book are matters of common human experience. All I have done is to go to the root of what they reveal, and to show that they can be related to opposite, yet from a more inclusive point of view, *complementary* cosmic polarities—the same polarities Chinese philosophy has named Yin and Yang.

Thus, basic human experience provides the foundation for what can become, potentially at least, powerful symbols evoking new possibilities in our lives. Unfortunately, however, most people are still unaware of the immense power of the symbols, and of the complex sequences of symbols forming the great mythos on which culture is always based. Perhaps most unfortunate yet, many young people grossly underestimate, or refuse to consider, the effect on what they call their 'personal' lives of the symbols of the culture in which they have been born and raised. Especially because of the transcendent character of the transpersonal approach to life I have been presenting, I have had to use symbols to convey its basic realizations.

Astrology is the main symbol I have been using. It deals with the central problem of human existence, because it refers to the most basic of all such problems: the meaning of the relationship between man and the universe of which he is a part. It does so because the *prima materia*, as it were, of astrology refers to the most primordial and universal of all human experiences (at least, as far as our present humanity is concerned): the experience of the sky in its day and night aspects, thus of light and darkness, of waking consciousness and sleep. What astrology essentially does is merely to interpret this experience of the sky. It can be, and always has been, interpreted in two ways: (1) the *symbolic and evocative* way, which sees in the whole sky and the ordered motions of the lights of Sun, Moon, planets, and stars a revelation of the order of earthly nature in as well as outside of man—and, (2) the *empirical and descriptive* way, which seeks to give a systematic formulation to the correspondence between recurring events in nature and periodic changes in the positions of an interrelationships among celestial bodies.

Today astronomy presents us with a picture of the sky fundamentally different from the ancient worldview. The human perspective has radically changed. We no longer think of the dualism of sky and earth, above and below. We are aware of the Earth as a planet within a solar system, which is but a small unit in an immense system of stars, the Milky Way Galaxy—itself in turn only one of apparently billions of galaxies. Whether all these galaxies are contained within a closed space, the universe, or whether they spread out into infinite space—we really do *not* know, even if many theories have been advanced.

Similarly, the validity of the picture of the constitution of human beings which our Western civilization had built on the foundation provided by the Hebraic and Greco-Latin tradition has been challenged in several ways since the mid-nineteenth century. The dualism of body and soul, of the human animal wedded to an angel, is giving way to the more complex concept of levels (or 'planes') of being—of consciousness and activity. Such a concept is the foundation for not only the new and transpersonal approach to astrology I have initiated, but also for a multilevel kind of psychology which I had envisioned a long time ago—particularly in a large, unpublished volume, *The Age of Plenitude* (1942)—and about which I have lectured in recent years. This approach to psychology was more specifically outlined in my most recently published book, *Beyond Individualism: The Psychology of Transformation* (Wheaton, IL: Quest Books, 1979).

This present volume not only adapts to astrological thinking and practice that multilevel approach to an understanding of Man (in the archetypal and non-sexual sense of the term), but it adds many new details to the formulations presented in *Beyond Individualism*. In this present book, the word 'astrologer' could in most instances be replaced by 'psychologist', for my approach to the immensely complex problems engendered by the mere fact of living in our city-dominated society transcends strictly defined categories of thought.

Understanding and, whenever possible, applying this multilevel approach is of paramount importance in any study of the development of societies and their cultures as well as of the growth of individual human beings. Every person, since birth, has been totally conditioned by the assumptions or beliefs of the culture in which he or she has grown up. The power of these assumptions and of the collective mentality formed by usually rigid religious, philosophical, or scientific concepts or dogmas is nearly as great as that of biological drives; and at times culture can overcome biology.

In the first chapter of this book, I have defined what I consider two basic ways in which human beings can meet the experiences of their everyday living. These two ways also refer to the characteristic spirit that pervades and ensouls a culture, its institutions, its basic philosophy, art-forms, and literature. At least for the last millennium, our Western civilization has powerfully stressed one of these two approaches to life, and in so doing it has produced *both* a spectacularly effective technology based on a relative mastery of material processes, and an increasingly ominous worldwide situation that could easily spell disaster. The other approach to life-situations and psychological problems is usually not well understood, because its character and implications have been presented in what, to our Euro-American mentality, seems to be a far too subjective, confusing, and naively symbolical manner by the men and cultures that have followed this approach. Symbols have, inevitably, to be used when trying to convey the meaning of this way of life, because it eludes precise intellectual and rationalistic definitions; but symbols can be used in different ways, and new ones more befitting the Western mind are now available.

Astrology today can, and I believe should, be considered a symbolic language—indeed a great *mythos* that could inspire and lead to much needed psychospiritual realizations many of the people who have recently been made to vicariously experience a totally new picture of the universe and the Earth, and who have acquired therefore a new sense of space and of cosmic organization. Technology has provided us with a distant view of our planet as a whole, experienced thus as the homeland of a humanity compelled, mostly against its will, to realize its fundamental unity in spite of constant international, religious, and ideological conflicts. But the science that produced this technology has not been able to create out of its discoveries symbols that could move and illumine the minds and souls of individuals, and still less of nations.

We need such symbols. Yet today only a small minority of vanguard minds are able to deal significantly with even symbols of the past, and attempts at creating new ones have mostly been failures or only temporary successes artificially induced by the media. Astrology, however, has kept spreading—but most of the time for superficial reasons. It has spread partly as a protest against the materialism and spiritual emptiness of our society, and against the academic institutions still hypnotized by the empirical method and the rigor of intellectual thinking— and partly as an escape from the responsibility of making decisions for which no rational reasons could be found for moving in one direction or another, so complex and filled with 'unknowables' our modern society has become.

Astrologers, eager to acquire an intellectual respectability and a legal status long denied to them, have sought to 'prove' the validity of their 'science' by empirical research and statistical methods; but in the meantime, modern science itself, especially since the revolution induced by Planck and Einstein, has increasingly become a symbolic language. A holistic approach is gradually challenging the atomistic character of 'classical' science. The worldview evoked by a new breed of 'philosophers of science' reaches far beyond the rational. Some of the most progressive and farseeing physicists are touching almost transcendent fields of existence and evoking through their complex mathematical symbols the feeling of the inter-relatedness of everything to everything else—a feeling that has been sung for centuries by mystical poets and interpreted in cosmic terms by great seers and occultists. The field is indeed being prepared at all levels for a planet-wide refocalization of human consciousness and a re-orientation of collective, as well as individual, hopes and desires. Astrology can play a significant role in the process—*provided* it does not cling to obsolescent 'classical' ideas and a kind of practice that does not help or inspire increasingly individualized and self-actualizing persons to transcend their old habits of thinking and feeling, and repolarize their energies.

Such a help is needed badly. People everywhere need understanding as well as guidance. They are confused by a multitude of options which they are unable to evaluate because they lack the required perspective and clarity of mind. The problem is how this needed help and guidance is to be given and, first of all, *on what basis?*

The only basis I can find practical and effective as well as philosophically—and even aesthetically—significant is a multilevel approach to the human being. In terms of cosmology, or 'cosmontology', this approach leads one to consider the universe as a hierarchy of fields of existence of systems of organization. It leads to the concept, not merely of 'holism' in the sense Jan Smuts used it in his seminal book, *Holism and Evolution,** But of what I have called *holarchy.*† In its application to human psychology and the future possibility of humanity's development, the

---

*(London & N.Y.: MacMillan Co., 1926).

†The philosophical and cosmological use of the concept can be found in my book*The Planetarization of Consciousness,* now in its third edition (N.Y.: A.S.I. Publishers, 1977). At the time I wrote the book, however, I did not use the term publicly. The term itself is used and ex-

concept of holarchy inevitably leads to the realization that a state of more-than-individual (or 'transindividual') existence is not only a possibility, but the only unglamorous, realistic and practical way to give meaning and direction to the presentday struggle of individuals and nations toward what many people, often naively, call the New Age.

The *possibility* of a really 'new' Age can be seen in the interrelated cycles of planetary and cosmic motions, if properly interpreted, but *cycles do not determine what will happen. They only evoke the possibility of the happenings and IF it happens, something of its basic character.* Man alone can decide what actually and concretely will happen—at least at Man's own level of existence.

Humanity is only a part of vaster wholes—the planet, the solar system, our galaxy—and these wholes hierarchically set the cosmic and planetary stages; yet, on the stage of the Earth's biosphere Man is a crucially important performer. Humanity no doubt has a role to perform, at least broadly defined by its place within these vaster wholes. The 'score' is not of Man's own making, but the performance is nevertheless his, for better or for worse; and every truly individualized human being is a responsible aspect of Humanity-as-a-whole. The whole acts not only *in* the individual, but *through* the individual. The whole realizes itself in and through the acts, feelings, and thoughts of its individualized participants who have become open to its descents of power. As this occurs, the transindividual state of existence is reached.

The way to such a state is what I call the *transpersonal path.* In no basic sense is it different from what esoteric traditions have spoken of as the Path of Initiation; yet this hoary and haloed word, Initiation, can be seen in a new light once the human being who is to tread the path leading to it has actually emerged from the chrysallis-state

---

plored from various points of view in other works of mine, for example, *We Can Begin Again—Together, Occult Preparations for a New Age* and *Culture, Crisis and Creativity,* as well as in my alreadymentioned most recent book, *Beyond Individualism: The Psychology of Transformation.*

of bondage to the particular culture that had formed his or her mind and conditioned his or her feeling-responses and behavioral habits.

Transpersonal astrology is astrology reoriented and repolarized to meet the needs of such individualized, or individualizing, human beings. It is not intended to meet the needs of *every* human being. It cannot be significantly and validly used by *every* astrologer; but neither should the controls of an atomic reactor be given to any college graduate having majored in ordinary physics. In the last chapter of this book I shall speak of the serious responsibility incurred by anyone using a truly transpersonal approach.

In closing this Prologue, may I stress the fact that *every* system of, or approach to, astrology may answer the need of, or fulfill a valid function for, at least *some* human beings. This is why a multilevel understanding of what is possible, meaningful to and especially required for a particular client is necessary. Moreover, at every level, the astrologer—and this applies as well to the psychologist and psychotherapist—can approach his or her relationship to the client in two basic ways. The choice of the way depends on the astrologer's temperament, training, and philosophy of living. Both ways can be valuable, depending on the circumstances and the character and state of development of the two persons involved in the consultation. What these two ways imply will be the first topic I shall consider.

This will lead to a study of the meaning, value and purpose of symbols. Then I shall attempt to throw light on each of the four basic levels at which the data provided by astrology can be interpreted. There must be different levels of interpretation because the consciousness and the energies of human beings can be focused at any one of these levels—and at times the focus of the consciousness oscillates from one level to the next.

Operating at the fourth level, however, is still for most human beings only a future possibility, and in the majority of cases a distant one at that. Yet, because mankind is today passing through a crucial crisis of reorganization and transformation, an increasing number of individuals, whether they are conscious of it or not, are seeking to work toward the concrete realization of this distant transindividual future.

For this reason, a greater understanding of what is involved in the transpersonal path of radical transformation is imperative. I can only hope that what I have written will assist those who are ready to gain such an understanding and to separate the possibilities inherent in our stage of evolution from the glamor and the ghosts of past eras.

# 1

## THE TWO BASIC WAYS OF MEETING LIFE'S CONFRONTATIONS

When human beings live at a purely biological, instinctual, animal-like level of existence, their reaction when faced with potentially harmful and/or painful situations is to adjust as smoothly as possible to what is happening, opposing a minimum of emotional resistance to natural events, flowing with the tide of change which they trust will once more bring favorable conditions. They do not feel separate from nature and its tidal and seasonal movements; and not feeling separate, they move inwardly with the change, instinctively following whatever path to safety presents itself to their alert senses and their opportunistic minds.

An automatic ability to effect needed readjustments is inbred in all living beings that unquestioningly and unconsciously fulfill their parts in the organic processes of the nature-whole to which they totally belong: the Earth's biosphere. Man, however, has within himself the capacity somehow to separate himself from the flow of events and ever-changing life-situations; he becomes aware that they happen to him—a 'him' that has a degree of objectivity and permanence within the flux of unceasing natural changes.

Man not only remembers his past experiences, but he is also able to communicate these remembrances to other human beings and to his progeny, and to the progeny of his progeny. In so doing he takes a stand that separates him enough from the happenings confronting him to enable him to observe the regularity of most of their sequences. He begins to interpret sequences of events and repeated series of experiences as 'entities' having a definite character. He 'names' these entities, and he is then faced with the problem of discovering and consistently carrying out the best, most secure and satisfying type of approach relating to these entities which—as we now realize—are personifications of what we call "forces of nature."

Some cultures reach maturity by stressing, sooner or later, the special ability human beings generically have to develop an objective and distinct awareness of natural forces and phenomena, and the will to *forcibly control* these in order to overcome the dangers and inclemency inherent in living in the biosphere. Other cultures, perhaps because of a more favorable, less hostile environment, as they reach a state of mature consciousness retain the *adaptive* approach which is fundamental in all pre-human species; but such cultures nevertheless constantly strive to transform this instinctual and primordial attitude by raising it to the level of a fully developed consciousness able not only to respond to the biological rhythms of human existence, but to resonate to the far more inclusive and clear vibrations of a higher Nature.

Most human beings are deeply and usually irrevocably conditioned by the general collective attitude and the great symbols or paradigms of the culture in which they were born and educated. Yet, especially in times of widespread crises of transformation, there are people who, either because of their temperament and parental inheritance or because they feel an innate urge to assert their independence from the collectivity, come to adopt a type of living reflecting a basic philosophy radically different from that of their ancestors. Because all over the globe at the present time of human evolution these cases have become very frequent and have given rise to deep-seated psychological problems, it is imperative for us to emphasize the existence of two basic ways in which human beings meet and respond to their experiences.

Our Western civilization, especially during the last five centuries, has officially accepted and powerfully implemented by a variety of social and cultural institutions one of these two ways: the way of forceful control or mastery over natural forces through a special use of the mind. Unfortunately, the intensity and exclusivism of this implementation may have now resulted in a potentially catastrophic world-situation; and, as could be expected, a strong reaction against the still deeply entrenched, official trend has begun to surface. The result has been characterized as a "revolution of consciousness." It is leading to an ideological struggle far deeper than the political 'cold war' between nations. It also manifests as a state of intense mental and spiritual confusion which has its repercussions upon all fields of human activity and consciousness —including the field of astrology.

In order to help dissipate this confusion, it seems essential to make as clear as possible the difference between the two basic ways in which human beings approach their everyday life-experiences and react to all kinds of meetings—meetings with complex social situations and unfamiliar facts as well as meetings with other people. These two ways can best be understood in their many implications if they are related to even more fundamental principles or polarities which can be seen operating everywhere and at all times because they are inherent in whatever can be said to exist. Existence, like electricity, is a bi-polar phenomenon. Long ago in China these two polarities were named *Yang* and *Yin;* and because these terms have recently been widely popularized in relation to the old book of oracles, the *I-Ching,* I shall use them to identify these most characteristic features of the two basic ways in which human beings act and react to either external impacts or internal changes. I shall briefly show how these two approaches affect the basic life-outlooks expressed in religions and philosophies and even in scientific theories concerning the nature of the world; and I shall also indicate how they condition the way astrologers look at the material they use and interpret the relationship between a person and his or her birth-chart.

I must, however, make it very clear that in using the terms Yang and Yin I am doing so according to their philosophical, cosmological, and psychological meaning, as I believe they were understood in the original Chinese tradition of the *I-Ching*. I am *not* using the words according to the Japanese system recently popularized in America and Europe as 'macrobiotics'—a system particularly associated in most people's minds with diet and food, even if it is also presented as a general way of life. This popular system may have validity; but it is hard to prove and justify classifying food and social attitudes as either Yang or Yin unrelated in practice to the original Chinese philosophical and cosmological concepts. In saying this I am not passing judgment on the Japanese system; I simply want to stress that in this volume, or any other of my writings, I am using the old Chinese terms in a way that does *not* correspond with their macrobiotic meaning.*

## The Yang Way

Yang type of activity is essentially outgoing, forceful, and aggressive. It is archetypally associated with the 'masculine' attitude and character. The basic Yang philosophy sees the universe as a stage on which force meets force, and at the biological level, most often fights against force. The Yang type of personality tries to use superior force to control, and in many instances, to dominate and subjugate whatever it meets, especially if a confrontation is involved which upsets the *status quo* or seems inimical to it. Whatever happens has to be controlled, then put to use in order to fulfill the needs, or often the personal wants and perhaps the greed or ambition, of the human being responding to the event.

Such a type of control requires the combined use of the mind in planning and the will in mobilizing the energies of the whole personality. When the individual deals with a repetitive situation and an either constant or periodic

---

*The word macrobiotic is a strange neologism, especially when applied to a very Japanese type of system. The combination of the Greek prefix 'macro' with the term 'bio' (meaning 'life') hardly seems significant. Life can neither be characterized as 'macro' or 'micro'. It is a polarized mode of energy which, for all practical purposes, is associated with conditions prevailing on a particular type of planet, but which has also been given a cosmic and metaphysical meaning as "the One Life" of a universe considered as an organism.

need or want which clamors for satisfaction, a *technique* has to be devised. The technique may be applied to the control of material energies and substances, of inner emotions, moods, or states of consciousness, or in ancient times, of astral entities or personalized forces of nature; in all cases, the mind is called upon to invent and precisely formulate the technique.

At the animistic level of tribal societies, the techniques of control had a radically different character from the ones used in our modern world. Yet both the medicine-man or shaman and the modern technician act in much the same spirit. They intend to make nature subservient to their wills. If the technique of the two types radically differs, it is because the human beings who formulate and apply them operate at two distinctly different levels of power, and their consciousnesses are structured by widely divergent philosophical and cosmological assumptions. These assumptions are derived from different ways of experiencing the world of nature—internal and psychic as well as external nature. A shaman—and some still exist under one name or another—perceives the universe and deals with what he experiences at a *biopsychic* level in his own characteristic, and to the academic modern mind, very *naive*, puzzling, and irrational manner. Our inventors, engineers, and technicians deal with another kind of universe whose nature reflects the character of the type of mind—the analytical intellect—our Western civilization has so strongly (indeed almost exclusively) developed since the 6th century B.C. and especially since the European Renaissance. The Western mind finds it easy to operate in a universe of physical matter which, because of its susceptibility to fragmentation, can be broken up by analysis and controlled by destructive agencies in highly concentrated form. As it is being destroyed, or rather *destructed*, we can observe matter dissolving into energy; but that energy operates at a level basically different from the one at which the shamans and true ceremonial magicians of old were able to exercise control and produce definite results. What they controlled is the life-power in its psychic and biological (or 'metabiological') operations. They were able to observe these operations thanks to special 'senses' (or perceptive agencies), just as modern physicists are able to trace the motion of subatomic particles in cloud chambers after the binding (or structural) power of atoms has been violently disrupted.

The atomic physicist gives a variety of names to unknown entities whose existence he infers from traces left on photographic plates; the magician spoke of various categories of 'elementals' whose existence he also inferred from their activity. The magician seemingly personalized these entities, giving them many names and projecting their structural character into hieroglyphs, magical seals or mantrams; but this personalizing approach is only superficially different from the theoretically impersonal methodology of modern technology. Magical formulas are not unlike the structural patterns of molecules, genes and atoms now in common use in chemistry and atomic physics. And different as the techniques are, *the intent* of these techniques is the same. This intent forcibly to control natural processes is what makes technique—any technique—necessary.

A technique implies that the technician has acquired 'knowledge'. Knowledge, however, requires objectivity and therefore a state of *separation* of the knower and the known. In a world which we basically experience as a process of unceasing change—as a constantly flowing 'river' of impacts and impressions within the limiting 'banks' of our senses and internal feelings—whoever seeks precise scientfic knowledge has, in some manner, to arrest the flow and isolate a moment of it for objective inspection; or else he has to record in some objective form a series of observations of *repetitive* events assumed to be 'the same'. Yet repetitive events are never the same *if* we do not isolate them from the context of the whole universe in which they occur, because this universe is always changing. We say that at the summer solstice the Sun rises at the same point on the Eastern horizon every year, but while it is the same point if we see it exclusively in re-ference to the relationship between the Earth's equator and the ecliptic, it is not the same point in cosmic space, for the solar system and the galaxy in which it is but a small speck, have been speeding away. *Nothing* is ever exactly in the same place in relation to the whole universe—unless we accept Nietzsche's concept of the 'eternal return' and thus refuse to think of infinity.

Knowledge is possible because we separate some facts from the whole universe and we freeze a particular moment of the vast process of universal change for precise observation. Such an act of separation implies a *resistance* to change, and all forms of resistance imply some kind of violence. By isolating a few variables under aseptic laboratory conditions, the modern scientist performs experiments which are even more separate from the universe. In the aseptic experiment, every possibility of intrusion of the universe into the laboratory is forcefully resisted against. What is the end result of such behavior? The possibility of a global suicide of mankind and an at least temporary destruction of the biosphere. Suicide is the logical end of a process of resistance to life. But such an end is an illusion—the great materialistic illusion. The universe always wins, because what is stopped at one level continues at another, from which it is eventually once more precipitated into a living organism at the level where the previous form of resistance had occurred.

I repeat that *knowledge separates the knower from what he or she wants to know.* Similarly, what I shall presently define as ego-centered and ego-ruled consciousness separates a particular 'field' (or area) of acceptable observation from the total possibilities of response to human experience. Such a separation is necessary at an early stage of human and personal evolution—in the childhood of both the human race and any member of it. It is necessary in order to make it possible for a particular center of consciousness—an individual—to discover, stabilize, and clearly define itself in terms of the feeling of being 'I-myself'. Definition at first implies exclusion, because to clearly formulate what one 'is' requires the realization of what it 'is-not'. But if the defined and stabilized conscious entity—or the logically formulated type of knowledge—does not come to understand or refuses to admit that it is part of some larger whole in which (consciously or not) it operates, then consciousness and knowledge become rigid and forcefully resist growth, evolution, and the universal process of change.

When a large rock is placed in the midst of a swiftly running river, a resistance to the flow of the water is generated; an eddy or whirlpool is formed. Some of the power of the current is deviated into that whirlpool. A human being similarly resisting life draws power from his resistance, but it is a tragic kind of power. In its extreme form it is the power associated with 'black magic'; and any violently egocentric and proud form of conscious resistance, if kept long enough, eventually turns into some kind of black magic, there being many kinds carrying other names and considered acceptable in a society having for centuries officially extolled a Yang way of life, a blatant or 'rugged' individualism.

To understand how this acceptance of egocentricity, aggressivity, and pride as a matter of policy has developed in the Western world, we should go back to its Biblical roots: the first chapter of *Genesis* in which God, having made Men in his image and after his likeness, blessed them and said unto them: "Be fruitful and multiply and replenish the earth and *subdue it and have dominion* over the fish of the sea, and over the fowl of the air, and over the cattle and over every creeping thing that creepeth upon the earth."* A literal interpretation of these words and of the concept of being a "chosen people" has pervaded not only Jewish culture, but the whole of Western civilization.# To this aspect of the Yang ideal of mastery or dominion, Greek culture added another as powerful incentive to the

---

*Genesis 1:28

#The esoteric meaning of this statement can only be grasped if we understand that the first chapter of *Genesis* refers to the creative process *at the level of Archetypes;* only the second chapter deals with the biosphere, the realm of material substances dynamized by the 'breath of life' into living organisms. In the first chapter, the Archetype 'Man' is created in both its male and female aspects. This Archetype 'Man' is a manifestation of Mind (in Sanskrit, *manas*); and Mind, in the essential meaning of the term, corresponds to the Element Fire. What God states is therefore that Mind-Fire is superior to and can transform by controlling the other three Elements: Air (birds), Water (fish), Earth (cattle and serpents). In the second chapter of *Genesis*, God has Adam — the concretized prototype (and no longer Archetype) of embodied man—give 'names' to every living thing he encounters. From the old magical point of view, by knowing the name of an entity, the entity

development of Euro-American pride (the 'white race' pride); the glorification of 'Reason' and of objective knowledge based on analysis and formalistic logic.

Western man thus developed as a worshipper of personal power, aggressive ambition as an elect of God, and the rational-intellectual mind. He felt, and in the great majority of cases still feels, empowered and selected by God to bring to the rest of mankind the 'blessings' of civilization and its by-products. The question here is not whether Western civilization has or has not brought great blessings to mankind, but whether the price paid for them has been so extreme that it is raising a strong possibility of bankruptcy—and, in a sense, fraudulent bankruptcy because of the means required for the development of these 'blessings'. No wise person should deny all value to the Yang approach to life; but also no really sane human being should find value in a nearly exclusive use of this approach. The universe itself will inevitably give rise to a reversal of the tide, for neither Yang nor Yin can be allowed to overpower the other beyond a certain limit. Existence itself depends on the balance of these two principles, and an extreme of disequilibrium is bound to lead to a compensatory reaction.

Such a reaction is now beginning. It is given a mythic character in the dream of a coming 'New Age'—an Age in which the Yin way of life will gradually assert itself and thereby bring about a transformation of mankind. What

---

can be controlled. But by so doing, Adam has separated himself from what he has named and he is 'lonely'. Then woman is created. In Hebrew she is *Isha*, and man *Ish*: the knowledge of the I-consciousness evokes its opposite, the intuitive faculty which (as we shall see in Chapter 5) brings to the ego promptings from the unconscious and dark area of the total psyche. Archetypal Man was meant to have control over the Earth Element (the things that creep upon the earth), but, when confronted with the power of that Element, the woman is said to succumb to it. In a sense, *Isha* refers to the nature of feeling which develops as a projection of the inner realization of being a separate 'I'. Through his feelings, man is drawn to the level of matter at which the principle of duality (the Tree of the Knowledge of Good and Evil) controls every activity. When mind becomes dominated by matter, it becomes the argumentative, either/or type of mind.

Cf. also my book, *Fire Out of the Stone* (Servire B.V., Holland: 1963) especially pages 123ff in regard to the above.

such a transformation implies and entails, however, is not clear to most of those who long for this New Age. To clarify what the Yin approach actually means, what it leads to and how it can be implemented in practice is therefore of the greatest importance today. To do so is evidently a most difficult and comprehensive task. All I can attempt here is to outline basic lines of approach, and to concentrate on the topic of astrology. This is a significant topic, not only because of its present popularity and the attraction it has for would-be devotees of New Age ideals, but because it reflects quite accurately the general state of personal restlessness and the confused thinking of the more dynamic groups of people who may be ready to experience a basic change of consciousness, even though still clinging at least unconsciously to the traditions of their now obsolescent culture. And it is to these people that all my work is addressed.

## The Yin Way

The Yin type of response to what life brings is essentially receptive and adaptive. It is archetypally associated with the feminine attitude and character. In a culture that upholds the Yin ideal, philosophers and wise men tend to consider the universe as an immense network of relationships linking and integrating a multitude of centers of consciousness and activity into a dynamic fullness (or pleroma) of being reflecting a transcendent and ineffable 'Unity' that can only be symbolized by inadequate names or concepts such as the Absolute, Space, an infinite Ocean of potentiality, or in religious terms, by God or the Godhead. While the Yang type of philosophy leads to a pluralistic, personalistic, and atomistic image of the universe, the Yin type is essentially holistic, seeing component parts of a cosmic Whole in every manifestation of a universal 'ocean' of life.

A Yin type of person is essentially characterized by its acceptance of what 'is', and by a willingness to experience every aspect of the ever-unfolding process of change. Such a person is thus free to meet whatever this process brings, and adapt to every new situation. A Yin type of person is primarily concerned with *the relationship* between the entities or forces involved in a meeting, rather than with what this meeting will do to his or her self or ego, because the person seeks to understand what function this relationship is meant to perform within a larger frame of reference—a family or community, a nation and its culture, mankind and the whole Earth, and ultimately the process of evolution of the cosmos.

Relationship and meeting are words that describe the coming together (convergence, commerce, or communion) of two or more spheres of consciousness and activity—two entities or persons—within a particular area of space; and space here may mean either the external space of a meeting of physical bodies or the internal space of the mind in which images and ideas are associated or in which they clash and refuse integration. Any meeting, in either kind of space, produces a 'situation'. The Yin type of person tends to be focused upon the *total situation*, whose meaning of the person tries to understand rather than to be concerned with his or her own reactions and those of the other parties to the meeting. Any event is seen as a 'meeting'. For example, if a person walking in a storm is struck by a falling branch, the happening would be interpreted as the meeting of the person and the tree. If attacked on a deserted street by a drug-addict in desperate need of money, this too is to be understood as a meeting. The respectable citizen and his attacker are performers in a situation for which, in different ways, both are responsible; the entire society is also responsible for the state of affairs which produced social conditions which gives this meeting its character.

Whatever the situation is—a boxing match, a Judo contest, a love affair, or baby-sitting with an aggressive child—the Yin-manifesting individual will not react to it instinctively or indignantly by trying to oppose superior force in an emotional outburst of violence and anger which might lead the attacker to use still greater violence. He or she will try to 'flow with' the situation, to adapt to what it implies. He or she will use 'intelligence', and intelligence is essentially the capacity to adapt to everchanging types of situations.

To adapt is, first of all, *to accept and not to resist the change*. It is, in the deepest sense, to try to understand the meaning of the happening. Why did the meeting occur between the attacker and the attacked? Why does the person who built a home near a river known to have flooded often find himself washed by the torrential waters amid the wreckage of his home? *Why?*

The search for meaning may come only after the experience is lived through, but the immediate reaction of the Yin-motivated individual is nevertheless one of essential acceptance of the meeting with whatever produced the crucial or painful change. I repeat that to such an individual the relationship between the experiencing self and the tormenting or disturbing factor— whether it be 'natural' or the result of personal enmity or social stress—is the essential element to be concerned with. And it may be a very pleasant meeting, 'love at first sight', or a deeply moving experience to which one normally would attach the qualificative 'spiritual'. In all cases, the experience is a meeting, even if it be the meeting of two biological or psychic or other (but equally 'internal') processes. The Yin-ideal of response to such a meeting is no longer 'mastery' but *sagesse* (a French word that has deeper implications than 'wisdom').

The Sage is not a 'master' in the Yang sense of the term; for the very word master implies *slave* as a referent— just as to be a mother implies having a child. The Sage uses control only in the sense of being in control of the aggressive and/or rebellious tendencies of human nature within his or her biopsychic organism, especially when this human nature has produced the solid, unyielding, and rigidly self-centered entity we call 'ego'. The Sage does not seek to exert superior force upon an attacking power; he does not live in a world where every change and event are interpreted as referring to a force-against-force situation— the world in which our modern Western science and technology exclusively operates. In that world even man's most superior mind and willpower is in the end always defeated. The Sage is not defeated because he seeks no victory. He does not fail because he courts no success and has no ambitions for achievement.

While the simple, natural, and instinctual type of human being displays a primitive and unconscious kind of *sagesse* in dealing with crises, he usually can do so only within a particular and well-defined set of situations. He is attached to the soil of the land of his birth, to his cultural ways of feeling and reacting, and to his personifications of natural energies as gods to be placated and worshipped. *The Sage is totally unattached to anything in particular.* He or she allows all life, all events, all human relationships *to pass through* his or her consciousness—indeed through the whole of his or her being at all levels of activity. The consciousness of the Sage could almost be called a 'sieve', for the vast flow of life's experiences pass through it; but the sieve *has form*, an individual form. It is a structured mind. What flows through it acquires *meaning*. This is the supreme mystery of *la sagesse*. It gives a meaning to everything that flows through the unresisting, yet totally focused, consciousness.

In this sense only can it be said that the experiencer and the experience 'are one'. The instinctual and intellectual reactions we call resistance vanish; where resistance was, meaning now arises: resistance is transmuted into meaning. In the same sense, one can describe an 'Avatar' as a field of activity through which cosmic or spiritual motion operates without any resistance. What in any human being is a subtle or crude form of resistance is, in the Avatar, *meaning*. The Act, the Actor, and the Meaning of the Act merge into a composite mystery that is both act and consciousness—at whatever level the action occurs—for it may be biological or cosmic activity. We may call it 'constructive' or 'destructive', but the name one gives simply reveals the specific character of the namer's resistance to universal Motion—his or her objectivity, and thus, separateness from the Act.

Where the Sage is, motion occurs. It is not even 'spontaneous' because spontaneity etymologically refers to what is 'one's own'. In the Sage, there is no longer any owner and only a release of dynamism which *is* consciousness at the center of the release. This center is the Sage; but it is not a 'he' or 'she'; it is simply the centrality of the motion, the 'tone' that is one of a myriad of overtones of the cosmic Fundamental of the field of activity to which the action refers. Quantitatively speaking, the existential field may be small, or an immense one of the planetary (or even galactic) scope. But quantity does not matter—or rather, quantity *is* materiality. At all levels (even at cosmic levels), the essential character of matter is resistance.

The Sage does not go after what we call knowledge, because, as I have already stated, knowledge is a function of resistance. In knowledge, something separates itself from its acts in order to analyze them objectively. But in doing this, what has become the object of knowledge is inevitably colored and affected by the subject (the mind, the ego) which immobilized it as an external and separate entity. In turn, the subject is likewise given a specious yet very definite character of objectivity by the very fact that as the one 'flow' of existence became arrested—thus resisted against—the observer and the observed were created as two distinct, objective entities.

Knowledge freezes the flow of universal Duration into moments that thereby acquire a particular character. They become particularities of what then becomes 'time'. Time, in this sense, is a quantitative, measurable factor which attaches itself to the Actor and Knower, for whom every experience becomes particularized because he or she has also become a 'singularity' in the universal whole. The Actor glorifies these time-particularities ('moments') into a mysterious, seemingly transcendent Now. But Now —at least as this now fashionable term is being used— implies a resistance to change.

The particularity (or singularity) can be expanded by the mind into a generality, but this hardly modifies its character; a small, limited resistance has become broadened into a *class* of resistances. Then, this type of resistance is related to a more or less large group (or set) of resisters. It no longer applies to one person, but to a psychological type, a nation, or a biological species.

True, 'wisdom', in contrast, is not based on an absolute separation between the experiencer and the experienced object, force, or entity. It brings the meeting to the state of *meaning*—a meaning which strictly refers to a particular situation and does not allow itself to be turned into a standardized and classified form of knowledge: the knowledge of what should be done by anyone whenever a situation appearing to have the same character occurs.

For the Sage, there is no 'whenever' and no truly valid categories of events, because every situation is a unique, unrepeatable meeting once it is referred to the universe as a whole within which it occurs; and as I have already pointed out, the universe never repeats itself. Its cycles are spirals, not circles; and in a still deeper, more transcendent sense, one should not speak of recurrence, because there are no fixed, rigid 'entities' to which anything happens. There is no meeting between self and not-self, because there is no separatable self, but only the one ultimate principle of Selfhood, SPACE, always in motion, yet never really changing. SPACE does not really change because its Motion is harmonic, ever-balanced; every movement is at once, timelessly, compensated for by another complementary movement.

The ideal of the Sage I have pictured may seem far beyond the reach of all but a very few human beings, but so is the ideal of the omnipotent and all-knowing Master. Both ideals are, like the two cosmic polarities of universal existence, Yin and Yang, unattainable in their absolutely pure states. They are ideals, not existential realities; yet they *point to* states of being, consciousness, and activity which may have an attractive and indeed compelling power, if an individual person has reached a stage in his or her evolution at which a deep-seated crisis demands an inner change of direction and a repolarization of the capacity for action and the mobilizing central will. Such a crisis may have only an individual character, but it may also occur in terms of collective, cultural, or political situations. It may refer to a seemingly isolated, even accidental event—as being attacked on a city street—but the situation may also be the end result of a long series of failures to act or of actions performed in a state of egocentric ambition, weakness of character, or attachment to obsolescent values and ideals, whether by an individual or a tribe, kingdom, or nation.

The Yin approach to a physical situation involving a sudden confrontation with a hostile force or person is the foundation of various Asiatic disciplines, often referred to as 'martial arts' yet having a much broader kind of relevance to interpersonal meetings in which one is faced by aggression, either moral or physical, mental or muscular. These disciplines are based on the principle of non-resistance and self-effacement formulated in Lao Tze's *Tao Teh Ching*. They teach the student to oppose 'space' (emptiness) to an external act directed against him. Becoming sharply aware of the physical place toward which this act is aimed, the student swiftly moves away from it, and the attack, finding only empty space, extends itself into a 'nothing' that forces the attacker into an over-extended and out-of-balanced position. The energy of the attack is used, as it were, to suck the attacker into a void where his strength becomes the power that defeats him and makes him fall.

Such a technique is more than mere technique, for it implies a basic reversal in the usual polarity of human consciousness. It does not refer to some procedure to be memorized by the mind after an analysis of the situation; it has to be an instantaneous and unself-conscious reaction in which the motive of the aggressive act one faces is negated. One does not resist the act, one accepts it and turns it against the attacker by refusing to be involved in it—thus by opposing to it only an inner void of response, by not being there (physically and/or morally and psychically) at the place the attack is aimed.

The principle of 'not-being-there' when confronted with violence so that the violence has no object to meet and thus to absorb or react to thrust, is what Gandhi meant by *ahimsa*, non-resistance and non-violence. This is the Yin principle to which the much misunderstood and presumably mistranslated words of Christ refer in the Gospel: "Agree with thine enemies." The word 'agree' should be understood to mean "do not use force against the force of the enemy and refuse to be the object of an aggression by 'not being there' where the aggresser expects you to stand."

An aggressor bent on attack will naturally aim at the point where a person is weak or unprotected. In such a situation, a Yang type of individual will rush reinforcements to meet the attack by opposing force to force. From the Yin point of view, this is senseless or at least exhausting; the consciousness becomes involved in the state of violence, and a long series of actions and reactions follow. What one should do is to refuse to be identified with that state of violence and counter hate with love, by opposing only space and emptiness (or egolessness) to the aggressive movement; thus, 'not being there' where the attacker expects a resistance to his attack. 'Not being there' may be physically impossible; but it is always spiritually possible, in the sense that a person being attacked may not be active in the situation *as an ego*. Even if the physical body suffers, the consciousness remains unaffected, secure in its own center and intensely aware.

The Sage meets such a type of situation according to the wholeness of what it implies. If he is weak, he accepts his weakness as he accepts the strength of the adversary. He understands the causes of this weakness and this strength, and is ready to let the energy involved in these causes exhaust itself. He transmutes what in him could have been resistance into meaning and understanding. He grows in wisdom through non-resistance against the karma of his past. By consciously allowing the dynamism of life—which is unceasing change—to flow through his consciousness and whole being, he is able to use this power of transformation as his own; yet, it is far more than 'his own', for he possesses nothing except the ability to centralize in consciousness and total understanding whatever *is*—all there is, without refusal and without exception—even the deepest darkness. He can calmly face this darkness, because he is unshakably centered in light. The only way to oppose darkness is to be more light. The vaster the space the consciousness illumines, the more it can afford to allow impacts of dark forces to enter and become lost in the light.

*Meaning* is produced by the relationship between opposites. In any attack or confrontation two opposite interpretations can be given. The aggressor has his own meaning for the aggression—an emotional and ego-centered meaning. If the intended victim reacts by also giving to the situation an emotional and egocentered meaning—fear, anger, hate—a cyclic pattern of action-reaction is built or strengthened, which sooner or later will call for more violence. But if the aggressor's attack meets only 'space', he eventually comes to see aggression as an empty gesture. The Sage has robbed it of its meaning; and however unevolved or hurt the attacker may be, he is 'human', and no truly human being can long hold even the crudest form of strength against the total loss of meaning in what he is doing. To live without the personal ability of investing one's activity with a meaning of what one's culture has considered meaningful, is spiritual death. It soon leads to actual physical death.

In the foregoing description of the Yang and Yin approaches to life's encounters and challenges, I have undoubtedly weighed heavily on the Yin side of the scale. The reason for this, as already stated, is that for centuries our Western society has extolled and glorified the Yang ideal and the practices derived from it.* As a result of this one-pointed concentration, spectacular material results have indeed been achieved, but they have nevertheless produced a situation in which violence has reached an explosive and perhaps uncontrollable character on a worldwide scale. Violence at the strictly biological level of existence and in terms of the satisfaction of the basic life-situations for self-preservation and self-reproduction has to be accepted as the law of the biosphere affecting all life-species; but when the human stage of planetary evolution is reached and the conscious mind and ego-will bring to these primordial drives a means to satisfaction

---

*In my book The Pulse of Life (written in 1942 and now published in a new edition entitled Astrological Signs: The Pulse of Life, Shambhala Publications, 1978), I studied the seasonal cycle of the year—the series of twelve zodiacal signs—in terms of the interplay of two forces which I called the Day-force and the Night-force. These two forces wax and wane in turn; they are of equal strength only at the two equinoxes. They correspond respectively to Yang and Yin. Our Western world is now historically at a point which should probably be located shortly after the maximum of the Day-force (Yang), when the Yin principle begins to wax in strength. In the year this would be shortly after the summer solstice. Is this why the symbolic and official 'birthday' of the United States is July 4? On the other hand, ancient India—structured by the Laws of Manu—is said to have been ruled by Capricorn, the sign of the winter solstice, when the Yin force, the collective factor, has maximum power. The spiritual individualism of Hindu yogis and seers would represent the complementary Yang-factor seeking to express itself. In America, the Yin-factor can be seen at work in the increasing dependence of individuals upon collective fashions of thought, feeling and behavior.

enabling them insatiably to increase the intensity and scope of their modes of operation, we are facing a most critical situation.

To fight against it in a Yang-like manner can only exacerbate the issue, even though a tendency to fight 'for the sake of righteousness' has been inbred in our collective mentality. We should rather meet the world situation—as well as personal situations in which the elements of conflict, impatience, jealousy, and gnawing frustration are so often present—with understanding and an unceasing search for meaning. And nothing in itself has meaning unless it be seen in relation to something else, and particularly in relation to its opposite. The deepest value of any action derives from the fact that it is needed to polarize another action of opposite character. The ultimate ideal is 'equilibrium'—a multi-directional balance of activities operating at several interrelated and interpenetrating levels.

Always activity. What makes it difficult for most people trained in our Western modes of thinking to understand the Yin way of life is that they associate this way with inaction and passivity. An unbalanced Yin type of attitude will lead to passivity and inertia, just as an unbalanced Yang attitude produces the ruthless, egocentric ambition and craving for any kind of exciting activity we often find in our present world. If it is difficult for us today to understand the character of the Yin type of activity, it is because we have been programmed to give value almost exclusively to the kind of behavior which brings to the ego the satisfaction of achieving what our senses can measure and our mind can manipulate in order to gain always more power *over* something or someone. Material results—and today this mostly means money and social connections—are considered almost the only proof of success in life, because no one can concretely measure and assess spiritual results.

Material results are possible because of the *divisibility* of matter. The achievements of modern science have been based on this characteristic of all material compounds which allows a full play to the operations of the analytical mind; and the ultimate products of this trend have been atomic fission and man's research into the behavior of the broken pieces of atoms he had subjected to an extreme of violence. 'Divide and conquer' is not only the motto of diplomats and politicians, it is also that of the man who seeks to rule all that is not himself. Today we speak glowingly of 'synthesis', yet this much abused term refers mostly to recombining in a new way what had first been atomized or pulverized.

Until quite recently, an 'atomistic' interpretation of the universe and all it contains has dominated science and the greatest part of philosophy. The opposite approach, 'holism'—a term first coined by Jan Smuts around 1920— is only now gaining a sudden favor, particularly among the still small minority of progressive thinkers and creative workers striving to build at least stepping stones, and perhaps foundations, for a much-idealized New Age.

It would be unwise, however, to identify the duality of 'atomism' and 'holism' with the Yang and Yin polarities of existence I have been discussing. These two pairs of opposites belong to two different conceptual levels. But it is evident that the Yang approach tends to develop an atomistic philosophy and cosmology; it pictures a world in which a fantastic number of 'billiard balls'—the atoms—are essentially distributed in a random manner, yet are also linked, pulled together or violently rushing away from each other according to the play of forces which in themselves have no meaning and no purpose. In such a world of 'force against force', individuals—atoms of human consciousness, egos—are supposed to be as indivisible as physical atoms were once thought to be. At the metaphysical and 'spiritual' level, these human atoms of consciousness have been called 'monads', each essentially separate and independent as well as immortal.

The world of holistic philosophers has an utterly different character. It is an immense Whole—and some say a supreme being or pantheistic God. This Whole cyclically differentiates in a multitude of parts which themselves are wholes having parts which are also wholes; yet the fundamental Unity is ever-present because every whole—large and small, atom, man or galaxy—is related to every other whole in an infinitely complex network of relationships. Through all these wholes, a unifying type of power flows which mystics and occultists, heirs to the traditions of the Vitalistic Age of mankind, have often called the 'One Life'. It is the life of the universal Whole that always remains essentially 'one', even though it superficially seems broken up into the myriad of little wholes that are but temporary condensations of the energy of Space—Space considered as fullness of being, consciousness, and harmonic activity (in Sanskrit, *Sat-Chit-Ananda*).

Atomism and holism are not the only two different and basically opposite ways of picturing the universe in terms of philosophical concepts and scientific procedures; these two approaches to 'reality' are to be found in nearly all fields of activity. They constitute two fundamental forms *consciousness* can take in coming to terms with human experience, just as Yang and Yin are the two poles, opposite yet complementary, of human *activity*. Both are needed in every field of experience that draws the attention of the ego—the 'I am' principle centralizing the field of consciousness and the motives for action. Yet one of the two polarities most of the time plays a decisive role, and in our individualistic and technological modern society the Yang principle and atomistic, personalistic, and achievement-oriented way of life are still so overwhelmingly in control that, in whatever field it manifests, the Yin approach seems to most people totally alien and incomprehensible.

The field of astrology is no exception. At least since the classical Greco-Roman period, astrology has been dominated by an analytical, personalistic, and fragmented type of consciousness, even though it dealt with concepts that once had integrally belonged to a vitalistic and profoundly religious system of beliefs. Today—particularly in America but also increasingly in Europe—two trends have developed out of the classical tradition mainly represented long ago by Ptolemy and more recently by 17th century astrologers in England, Germany, and France. One of these trends is oriented toward the development of a 'scientific model' for astrology through the use of empirical research and statistics. The other trend has sought to align astrology with the remarkable transformation of Western psychology since the days of Freud, particularly since the work of Carl Jung and the subsequent growth of 'Humanistic psychology' with Abraham Maslow, Anthony Sutich, Carl Rogers, Rollo May, et al. Because it soon became clear that the Humanistic and Human Potential movements have their limitations, a new trend developed along lines related to a growing interest in parapsychology and mystical experiences, and the term *transpersonal* was used to characterize this entire field of psychological investigation of what seemed to be at the borderline of consciousness.

At about the same time, I realized that the development of an almost exclusively psychology-oriented and 'humanistic' astrology, which the publication of my book *The Astrology of Personality* in 1936 had stimulated, was still following, in most instances, a mainly descriptive and strictly informative line. This realization led me a few years ago to initiate and formulate in general terms a transpersonal type of astrology.

This transpersonal astrology is meant to meet the often largely unconscious need of a vanguard of individuals who are now feeling—at times almost compulsively—moved to seek a type of guidance and inspiration that would throw light upon a process of radical transformation they believe necessary for them to go through because of their eagerness to become pioneers in a New Age and a new life. It is true that in the distant and recent past much has been written by the mystics and occultists of all cultures concerning such a process of human metamorphosis; but what had been said can be more confusing than helpful to the modern minds of individuals who now start from a point totally different from the starting point of Asiatic or even old European aspirants. The Yin approach to life which forms a background for this transpersonal orientation is still completely foreign to the typical Western mentality; and the religious language in which 'the Path' was described in the past is so difficult for academically trained individuals to assimilate [merely memorizing its terms is not enough] that the outcome of the search is often either a repeated state of frustration and disappointment, or a binding subservience to the outer forms of disintegrating cultural molds.

In dealing with this Yin way of life, symbols have to be used, because our Yang-oriented modern languages become awkward and confusing for the purpose of guidance on the path of radical transformation, not only of consciousness, but of our motivations for action. Just as the symbols of higher mathematics and group-algebra have proven necessary for an understanding of the non-rational series of events following the violent release of nuclear particles once the structure of the atom is forced to break down, so astrology, as a strictly symbolic language, can be used to bring a sense of order and sequential meaning to events and the inner experiences of individuals who have consciously taken upon themselves the momentous and dangerous task of transforming all the implications of human existence in their own lives, or who have been unwillingly caught in a maelstrom of social disruption. Astrology can also help the individuals who expect a new departure in human affairs to discover the cyclic meaning of the worldwide series of events which have marked our tragic century and to place their own expectations in a correct time-perspective.

Nevertheless, astrology can confuse the seeker with an insignificant and unconstructive mass of information and a plethora of data having no relevance to the basic process of transformation. The traditional interpretation of these data may even distract the attention of the aspirant and take him or her away from the straight-and-narrow-path eventually leading to a 'transhuman' state of existence, by inducing him or her to find easy solutions to life-problems in ancestral attitudes defined by simplistic or overly-abstract concepts.

In the following chapter I shall therefore try to establish a clear contrast between two basic approaches to astrology and between two interpretations of generally used astrological data so that the alternatives are made as clear as possible. Then the reader will be better prepared to deal with what is involved in the practice of transpersonal astrology.

# 2

# THE TWO FACES OF ASTROLOGY

Before I begin to discuss the two basically different approaches to astrology I have mentioned, I should try to clarify what actually constitutes astrology and what it is *for*. Most simply defined, astrology is an apparently successful attempt to establish a complex set of consistent and reliable correlations between, on the one hand, the observed motions of apparent sources of light in the sky — Sun, Moon, planets, and stars—and, on the other hand, equally observable series of changes occurring within the biosphere and, particularly, in the lives of human beings.

Such a definition does not present any *interpretation* either of what moving dots or discs of light across the sky actually are, or of the kinds of changes astrology relates to them. It does not try to explain why and how such correlations operate. It simply says that two sets of factors—one celestial, the other terrestrial—can be correlated, and that establishing such correlations seems to be valid inasmuch as it has been a consistently pursued endeavor wherever and as long as human beings have been able to use the mental (or psychic) processes it requires. But what has been the purpose of this endeavor?

The purpose of astrology is to use the above-mentioned correlations in order to understand the repetitive order observable in the processes of change experienced by all human beings living in the biosphere and the meaning of what occurs during these processes—so that, as the result of this understanding, human beings may increase their ability to cope with and benefit from the changes they experience.

It should be evident that, thus stated, this purpose of astrology can take different forms according to the level of consciousness and general character of the main activities of the human beings seeking such an understanding. With experiences limited and strictly defined by the narrow boundaries of the land on which primitive communities lived and to which they were biologically and psychically bound, tribal man used astrology primarily for agricultural or cattle-raising purposes. The *interpretation* he gave to the discs and dots of light he saw in the sky was conditioned by a type of consciousness operating in terms of animistic religious beliefs; it was essentially different from that of a 17th century European astronomer using a telescope in an observatory. It even differed from the interpretation which led colleges of priest-initiates in Chaldea or late Egypt to build complex astrological systems pervaded with the imagery of intricate religious myths, and in many instances with concepts derived from occult and/or magical practices.

Today the recent discoveries of astronomy and the use of new means of perception have induced, or at least are gradually inducing, an understanding of the universe radically different from that of Galileo and Newton. Astronomy has made a jump from the solar system to the galaxy and beyond; and the strictly mechanistic, atomistic, and rationalistic character of 'classical' physics is now superseded by a transcendent and symbolic approach to physical reality, the meaning of matter and even of universal laws. As a new level of consciousness is being reached, an equally new type of interpretation of the celestial factors used in astrology inevitably has to follow, even if most people interested in astrology find it difficult consistently and effectively to think in terms suggested by the recent developments in nuclear physics, astronomy, and parapsychology.

The new type of interpretation presented to us by astronomy calls for what I have called a transpersonal approach to astrology. Such an approach contradicts in no way the fundamental definition of astrology I have formulated above; we merely have to give a relatively new interpretation to *both* what we can now observe in the sky with complex astronomical instruments and our generically human and individual experiences. On the one hand, the celestial phenomena our forefathers could only perceive with the naked eye are now understood and evaluated in relation to immensely larger formations whose physicality becomes questionable once matter is seen as merely a special state of energy; and on the other hand, the changes human beings are now experiencing—not only individually but collectively and on a planetary scale—are of such magnitude and so full of unparalleled opportunities for growth and transformation that they can be significantly interpreted only in terms of a far more inclusive frame of reference.

The fact is, nevertheless, that just as a vast majority of the people of the world cannot comprehend the world-picture of the most progressive 'philosophers of science' and nuclear physicists—or the writings of great mystics and true occultists—so they cannot feel, think, and behave in terms of an ideal of life that would basically transcend their strictly personal and ego-centered interests, and even what they believe is their 'spiritual' (yet very 'personal'!) concept of growth. They can accept changes of attitude only from the perspective of greater personal health, wealth and happiness—a perspective not essentially broadened by the newly fashionable goal of what is usually understood as self-actualization and creativity.

There is, however, nothing wrong with an ego-centered type of consciousness and activity. It simply marks a particular stage in human evolution. The liberal idea that all men operate at the same level of consciousness is patently fictitious. At least today, human beings undeniably operate at several levels of emotional, mental, and spiritual development. Even though the outer circumstances of their lives may be utterly different from those faced by archaic man in the jungle or desert, truly 'primitive' human beings can still be found in all countries, and not merely in New Guinea or other remote regions. In some parts of India, a most rigid type of tradition-worshipping brahmins live side-by-side with thoroughly Westernized Indian Ph.D.'s and spiritual revolutionaries like a few disciples of the great seer-philosopher Sri Aurobindo and his co-worker Mother Mira.

There is no absolute *Truth* or *Value* when applied to the life of an individual, only what, for that individual, is the fulfillment of his or her *dharma*—that is, of what his or her birth-potential allows to be actualized. There assuredly is, in every human being, a potential for self-transformation, for becoming *more* than what he or she is, according to the standards of the culture and period in which he or she was born; but the process of transformation has always to start from a particular level of sociocultural normality.

One should not ignore the character and limitations of this level, for they condition the all-important starting point of the process. The inner pressure of the initial phase of a life-process represents the *karma* which the process has constantly (or periodically, stage after stage), to overcome. The spiritual Teacher or Guide, in one sense, provides the aspirant to transformation with an ideal Image of a higher evolutionary phase of the process. While the Guide's task is to impress this Image upon the consciousness of the one he or she helps, it is also to make very clear what is demanded of the aspirant in order to take *the decisive step* from the past to the future level of conscious development required for the actual transformation. Dharma can only be fulfilled when a one-pointed effort is consciously and willfully made to meet and neutralize *the karma that had set the stage for the start of the process of transformation.*

It is therefore very important for anyone who is seeking or dreaming of a 'transpersonal' process—whether in the strictly psychological or the astrological field—to have a clear idea of what the personal stage means. It is necessary indeed for whomever claims to work for an often overly-idealized and utopian New Age to understand what are and, from the start, have been the characteristic limitations of the Old Age he or she is so eager to leave behind. If this is not done, the Old Age will inevitably retain its grip upon unconscious and repressed areas of the collective psyche of the would-be New Ager.

For this reason, even at the risk of establishing too clear cut distinctions between what are actually gradually transitions, I feel it necessary to attempt to define four basic levels at which astrologers can interpret *both* their individual and collective experiences and needs, and the celestial motions from which astrology derives the raw materials for its interpretations, its predictions or great symbols of transformation. These levels — as we shall see — can be characterized as the *biological*, the *sociocultural*, the *individual-personal* and the *transpersonal*.

However, before I attempt to outline in some detail what the operation of the consciousness at each level brings to the interpretation of astrological factors being used, I have to state and to some extent develop a basic fact directly related to what I have discussed in the preceding chapter. At each of these four levels, astrology can be used for two basically different kinds of purposes. These two purposes can be related to the two basic ways of meeting life-confrontations already described — the Yang and the Yin ways. According to the Yang way of approaching the interpretation of astrological data, the astrologer seeks *to gain information*, and as a result, *knowledge*. On the other hand, the Yin approach is essentially for the purpose of *developing understanding*, and as a result, a realization of meaning. Through knowledge comes a certain type of power, power related to the knower for him or her to use. Through the realization of meaning, a human being can obtain wisdom, or more accurately, *sagesse* — a special quality of openness of living in a full and positive consciousness of being.

## 1. An Astrology of Information

The word *information* has lately become a keyword because the passion for new data and the classifying of these data, called facts, is one of the dominant traits of the modern technique-worshipping mentality. The 'how to' books sell by the millions in a society in which knowledge is most often equated with the possession of computer-izable information and memorizable recipes. In order to be made available, information has to be recorded in some manner. It is recorded by means of *signs*.

Anything that conveys definite information to someone can be called a sign if it deals with a fact or series of facts belonging to the level of reality that the person being informed can perceive, comprehend, and become actually related to. A road sign informs the driver of a car that definite conditions on the road can be expected, or that a particular type of behavior is required (slowing down or a special state of watchfulness), or that a definite number of miles have to be traveled before a particular city is reached. When a new machine or drug is bought, the buyer usually receives with it information concerning the use of what was bought. Words which describe a person's behavior or the shape and color of an object in terms of perceptible data are also signs. If, however, instead of clearly indicating precise features the words can and are meant to only *suggest or evoke* states of consciousness and feeling, or the presence of supersensible forces or conditions, such words become *symbols* — and I shall presently define the meaning I give to this term, symbol, and its implications.

Signs fulfill a most basic need in any social mode of existence: the need for communication among the members of a community, or eventually of a *particular*, even if widespread, culture. The more complex the society, the more precise the means of communication must be; the more any doubt as to what the signs indicate must be eliminated, and, therefore, the more technical the character of the information. In our very complex and largely artificial kind of society, demanding the use of ever more intricate techniques, human beings have their attention constantly aroused by a multitude of signs or indicators. Nearly every change of situation we are to meet has been catalogued and described by specialists in factual, clear-cut terms. We live in terms of a 'knowledge' of what we are to expect—in terms of precise sequences of causes and effects. When the word 'meaning' is currently used, it refers to the strictly defined 'indication' of what can definitely and unquestionably be known about something—something from which the knower is separate as an observer or a detached operator.

This kind of knowledge is communicable to everyone whose mind is able to learn and memorize the rules on which it is based and learn what the signs indicate that were used for the communication. When astrology is used strictly as a means to convey definite information, it is also considered to be such a form of knowledge. The position of a planet in a particular zodiacal sign or natal house, or its aspect to another planet, is known to indicate a variety of definite conditions or events. The 'knowing' is traditional, inasmuch as it is based on transmitted records of generations of astrologers who (it is believed) established and checked the validity of the indications. It is memorized as well as consensus knowledge. We may also call it 'factual' knowledge, and prove its validity by impressive statistics. The question one must ask is, however: what does the word *fact* indicate?

Etymologically this word refers to something being 'made' (*factum* in Latin). What a person experiences may or may not be accorded the status of being a 'fact' by other members of his or her society and culture. This status relies upon the common acceptance *within a particular culture and at a particular time of history* of the personal experience of all people supposed sane, or at least sufficiently trained or intelligent to be able to pass judgment. To the extent to which an individual's experience differs from the experience of the people of his culture, his or her 'facts' may be considered by them to be fantasies or psychotic illusions. They fall outside of the field of knowledge of the community. If they are taken seriously by some people, it is not as 'facts' and as 'signs' indicating some aspect of a commonly perceptible and intelligible reality, but instead as 'symbols' *evoking the possibility of the existence of another kind of reality.* Facts do not have in *themselves* an evocative character; if for some people they have such an evocative character, they have become symbols.

These two words—sign and symbol—should be clearly differentiated from one another, otherwise different fields of experience, different levels of consciousness and different kinds of use are unintelligibly mixed; and the inevitable result is a confused mind. Similarly, when astrology claims to be able to state that every position of and relation between celestial objects indicates a clearly definable event or character trait, such a kind of astrology deals with 'signs' (indicators) conveying more or less precise information, but not with 'symbols'. The astrologer who considers astrology a symbolic language whose function is to evoke possibilities of changes in the process of growth and transformation which is human life, and to deal with the meaning of the successive phases of this process from birth to death, cannot logically use, according to set traditional rules, astrological data as indicators of knowable facts. In other words, the consciousness of this astrologer and that of the followers of 'classical' astrology operate at two different levels. Both levels, I hasten to say, can be considered valuable. Each is valuable *if* it answers the need of the person asking for astrological advice or guidance. As we shall see later on, the most difficult problem confronting an astrologer—or in his own field, any psychologist—is how to become aware of what the need of the seeker is, and what his or her consciousness is able to respond to and wholesomely assimilate.

Valuable as both approaches undoubtedly can be, it would be, I believe, very unwise to underestimate their differences. They are differences not only in the technical aspects of the practices, but also differences in the temperaments and mentalities of the astrologers who are inwardly impelled to follow, or at least find themselves more at ease in following, one mode of interpretation or the other. The great majority of college-educated people all over the world have been trained to depend almost entirely on precise technical procedures and memorized interpretations of specific data or factors essentially separate from each other.

For example, most astrologers take for granted that each planet has a definite character which it retains in all circumstances, somewhat as a human being is believed to have an inalienable and basically unchanging individuality. This is the atomistic approach. But the astrologer who holds a truly holistic position sees a planet as a symbol of a function which has meaning in terms of the whole solar system and, therefore, is fundamentally involved in a web of relationships with other planets. Similarly, such an astrologer approaches and deals with his or her clients in relation, if not to humanity, at least to their community and culture, whether they passively accept, rebel against, or are quietly determined to overcome the pressures and question the value of the models that culture or community always seeks to imprint upon all its members.

In the first case—the atomistic approach—the astrologer deals with 'signs' or indicators which always retain their basic character. The positions of these indicators — planets, nodes, midpoints, Parts, etc.—provide the astrologer with more or less clear-cut, yet theoretically reliable, information; and if the astrologer is scientifically inclined, statistics can be used to prove the validity or scope of the information. The client can therefore be given this information, possibly with a nicely scaled list of probabilities for the future. What the client feels about the information, how he or she will be able to handle or assimilate it, does not bother the astrologer very much; all he or she may try to do is to stress the positive rather than the negative implications of the 'facts'—the objective information given by definite data whose traditional or statistically demonstrable validity is more or less established.

Such an atomistic astrologer behaves like any scientist or technologist normally does. The scientist discovers a 'law', analyzes the components of a particular situation, and with no great interest in the ultimate consequences of what he has discovered, simply formulates a 'truth' which the technologist-engineer will apply, if he can profit from the invention, or if he is paid by a firm to create new and sellable products.

Such an analysis of the astrological situation (when approached along the lines of objective information and technical discovery of what are considered facts and laws), may seem to many students or fans of astrology rather crude and unsympathetic. This was, nevertheless, exactly the way in which astrology was practiced in America before a more psychologically-oriented approach developed *after* the 30s of this century.* A good astrologer

---

*This is still the way astrology is practiced in India, in most of Europe and even in America.

did not have to meet the client, whose life-circumstances he or she usually did not know or care to know. Merely on the basis of the time and place of birth the astrologer had to provide information as to what was going to happen to the person, what profession was indicated in the chart, what the financial and health situation would be, etc. To this, later on, was added an expected analysis of 'character' and the 'strengths and weaknesses' of the person writing or personally asking for information.

This kind of information is in no way different from what General Eisenhower, planning the Normandy invasion in 1944, asked of weather experts and intelligence officers. The General then had to make his decision according to the facts he was given. He and his army were completely separate from these facts, just as for a traditional astrologer the client is separate from his or her birth-chart—an immortal, rational soul finding itself in an essentially alien situation on this earth in order to "learn some lesson" or to "work out his or her past karma," then to "return home" at death.

In saying this I am not passing judgment on the validity of such an approach and of the religious or metaphysical premises on which it is founded. It has been, and in many places for many people still is, the traditional and official approach. The consciousness of these people has been formed by it, and they may be able to respond only to it. What I am merely stating is that another approach is possible, and that today the specific character of the time and of the 'human condition' makes the determined and insistent actualization of such a possibility a matter of crucial importance. It is, I believe, of crucial importance in all fields of human activity; and astrology today has become a significant field because it answers a basic need of modern men and women: the need for a new meaning to their lives. To impart this meaning, symbols are required, great symbols that—now as in all periods of human development—are integral parts of human experience and in their togetherness and interrelatedness constitute a profoundly meaningful *mythos.*

## 2. An Astrology of Understanding and Meaning

The words *understanding* and *meaning* are, unfortunately, generally used with little or no concern for what they should most characteristically refer to. 'Understanding' basically differs from 'knowledge', and 'meaning' differs from 'indication'. Strictly speaking, 'knowledge' is transmitted through 'signs'; and 'understanding' through 'symbols.' Knowledge implies a separation of the knower from the known. Knowledge is objective, while intuition is subjective. To understand, literally, is 'to stand under'—thus to feel the weight and experience the 'roots' (or causes) of what is being understood. We should not say that we understand a sign; we either know or do not know what it indicates. If we are asked whether we have met a person, we might answer, "Yes, I know him." We would not say, "I understand him" unless we are aware of his character and the basic way he usually acts and reacts. A scientist knows many things he does not actually understand.

Facts are observed and known; symbols should be understood if their meaning is to be 'revealed', and understanding a symbol should always involve to some extent 'feeling with' the culture or group of persons that raised a mere fact to the level of a symbol. We know as a fact that some criminals in old Palestine were crucified and adulterous women stoned. But the image of a crucified Christ in a Catholic church is not there merely to indicate an assumed historical fact, but as a poignant and potent symbol of a way of life, an ideal of supreme sacrifice and compassion. A fact is only what it is; it can be precisely defined. A symbol is far more than what it portrays, for it not only represents a single situation; it points to a complex group of feelings and values. A symbol is not an indicator; it is at least potentially a revelation of meaning and, through meaning, of an implied purpose.

Symbols integrate the separate experiences and aspirations of many people, and they are the foundations on which a collectively accepted culture is built. Symbols take events and facts out of the realm of the unique and the fortuitous—the realm of incomprehensible, meaningless chance and random activity—and into the realm of 'universals', and of collectively valid principles and motivations. Symbols enable us to come to terms with situations we can only meet fully and meaningfully on the basis of collective experience and a collective set of values. Symbols arise out of the common experience of human beings in answer to a need they all, consciously or unconsciously share. But there is a hierarchy of human needs; some are more basic and common to all men, others are experienced only by individuals facing the possibility of some deep internal transformation, or of a radical change in their outer life.

When Gautama the Buddha came to the people of India, he became the Exemplar of a way of life and a type of mentality that masses of human beings needed—human beings who had long been subservient to a rigid caste system and forced to follow an endless series of rituals controlled by a powerful Brahmin caste. The image of the sitting, meditating Buddha came to be the symbol of a new kind of wisdom and detachment which he had made available to anyone willing to follow his 'middle way' and his practice of a few basic virtues in order to reach a new level of mental functioning—a new wisdom.

In Europe, the crucifix became the symbol of another approach to life emphasizing the feeling of love and devotion, and preparing human beings to meet their most transforming crises through total surrender and sacrifice and thus to reach an eventual rebirth into a higher realm of being—the Resurrection symbol.

The lives of Buddha and Christ were made into 'myths' (or mythos). Every event in these lives was raised to the level of symbol releasing a universal or archetypal meaning, an example to 'imitate'. The religions built upon these symbols and archetypes ritualized the many aspects of these great myths, and many more symbolized phases of the process which their devotees were led to experience as they sought to 'identify' themselves with the idealized image of the God-impersonating or divinely inspired being.

Astrology can also be understood as a great and (in the past) universally accepted *mythos*. What this *mythos* pictures and seeks to reveal in the most impressive manner possible—i.e., by predicting the future—is simply the *orderliness of the universe in which human beings live*. By so doing, astrology fills the most basic need of human beings, the need for order and security. For this reason, astrology has rightly been called 'the mother of science' and indeed of civilization, because science and all manifestations of culture (religion included) cannot exist unless human beings can *feel* that whatever kind of rules and social regulations they devise to structure their collective social life in some way reflect (or imitate) a universal order. The belief in the existence of such a universal order arose in the earliest days of human evolution on this Earth when human beings were able to experience not only the day-and-night rhythm and the periodicity of the seasons, but also the amazing spectacle of clear night-skies and the repeated and reliable rise and setting of the brightest stars at certain times of the year.

Astrology has always been, basically, a religion founded upon the daily, monthly, and yearly ritual performed by stars, Moon, and Sun. Anyone even slightly acquainted with pre-Christian cults of the East-Mediterranean and Near-Eastern world, and with the Mysteries, has heard about the 'solar myth' and the trials, death, and rebirth of a 'solar Hero' symbolizing the descent and reascent of the 'Soul' of Man. But actually, the Sky itself was the scene of the cosmic *mythos*. The sacred Mysteries were only reflections of what occurred in that part of infinite Space visible to human beings. To make the cosmic ritual of planets and stars and of the two Lights (Sun and Moon) experienceable, so that human beings could identify and 'feel' themselves with its cyclic events, the Mysteries were founded. Astrology, when used at the level of the individual person, is actually a particular application of the Mystery concept.

We should never forget that modern science, with all its sophisticated instruments, gives us only the *image* of the universe our modern consciousness is able to picture. It interprets what man can perceive, directly or through his instruments—*only* what man perceives. We do not know what ranges of vibrations exist below and above our perceptions. What we call reality is *our* human reality—a projection of the limited awareness we have of what *is*. The modern universe of galaxies and metagalaxies is as much a 'myth' as that of the Ancients who saw, in what we call stars, the bodies of hierarchies of creative gods and, in the Milky Way, the womb of Souls. An imaginative scientist, Donald Hatch Andrews, wrote in his beautiful book, *The Symphony of Life*, that the world is more like music than matter, because everything in it is now, for us, resolved into vibratory frequencies. A classical European symphony is also a myth—a structured organization of sounds and thus of vibrations. Back of all these myths is man's essential need to believe that he lives in a world of order and—most human beings are compelled to add, in order to experience life sanely and securely—a world of meaning. Even if we cannot fathom or understand what the meaning essentially is, we have to believe such a meaning exists, and that the cosmos is an organic whole—a structured and harmonic system of immensely varied and complex but balanced activities.

Only embittered and proud human beings whose nervous systems and minds have been shocked by catastrophic and *to them* incomprehensible series of events can assert with the post-World War II Existentialists that the world is absurd, and that man alone is able to stand in the midst of this absurdity with the (to them) sublime power to project his own values and selfhood upon an infinite space filled with the meaningless motion of randomly produced aggregations of material atoms. But even such a tragic and senseless world-picture, and that of a forever identical 'eternal return' of which Nietzsche dreamt on his way to actual insanity, were attempts to create a *mythos*, the only one with which its human creators were able to live significantly. These myths represented *their* personal answer to the need for order. Even disorder can be understood as a form of order, for negation is only an affirmation of the refusal to accept and conform to *any* positive statement *known* to the mind which denies.*

This does not mean, I repeat, that astrology cannot validly be used also simply as a tool to give a particular and valuable kind of information. This is its empirical and, in the broadest sense of the term, scientific aspect. In the distant past among agricultural or cattle-raising tribes, astrology was certainly practiced to convey biological information. It can also today be used at another level in an attempt to analyze and describe the temperament and character of a person, and thereby add *another dimension of knowlege* to the practice of clinical and analytical psychology. The basic question I have been raising for many years is whether such an approach to astrology answers *the most fundamental need* of restlessly seeking and future-oriented men and women who have already consciously and deliberately entered upon a path of radical transformation, or who, most unconsciously and uncertainly, have taken hesitant and unsteady steps in that direction. These individuals seek far more *trans-formation* than *information*. They long for a clear vision of what is possible for them and what their entire life-pattern might mean as a process of metamorphosis, rather than traditional pat answers to the usual type of problems of day-by-day living.

---

*In Medieval occultism, the Devil was said to be God inverted; and in *Faust* Goethe characterizes Mephistopheles as he who always denies. However, many a student of esoteric doctrines sees in 'Lucifer' literally a 'Bearer of light'. This 'Luciferian' light is believed to represent a rebellious refusal to accept the inertial rule of an 'old' God. But the basic question is whether this refusal to conform is *only* engendered by Satanic pride and without any new and more inclusive vision of order to give it a positively future-oriented character, or whether it is founded upon a Promethean desire to begin a new cycle that will sooner or later reveal a higher field of consciousness and thus a new and greater reality.

Today, the rebelliousness of a youth dreaming of a utopian New Age has often actually a Satanic rather than a Promethean character. In its extreme form it has led to terrorism. In its mild state it manifests as a confused and often drug-induced condition of unfocused consciousness recalling the famous 'melting pot' ideal of our American society. A melting pot is not a 'synthesis'. It is chaos, not seed. The future is latent within the seed, not in the undifferentiated humus produced by the decay of leaves, even if both humus and seed are needed to produce new life.

I certainly am not alone in insisting that mankind today is in dire need of a new *mythos*, and of a reawakening of 'the sense of the sacred'. Such a need implies the realization that life, when lived in terms of meaning and purpose, is basically to be considered a ritual or, in more modern terms, a structured process whose every phase is filled with significance. This significance cannot be known as the result of a set of information or recipes; it can only be evoked by symbols whose deepest meaning has to be intuitively experienced through the interpenetrating activity of the mind and the feelings—for this meaning is both objective and subjective, transcendent, and immanent. Such an activity of *thinking-feeling*—clear and deep organismic feeling—has a sacred character. It is both holistic (for it involves the whole being), and creative (in the sense that it raises the possibility of beginning a new phase of the process of ritualistic living).

In a collective tribal-cultural sense, any creative rebeginning is a *reflection* in the personal life of the one Creative Act of the gods, or God. Thus everywhere man has imagined a 'Creation Myth' as an eternal (ever-repeated) and sacred (divine) model and inspiration for all the great moments of rebirth that may be experienced, at first, by the tribe as a whole and, later, by a group of dedicated and even consecrated followers of a 'great religion' celebrating a yearly series of festivals. Today—as human beings have increasingly developed a sense of individuality and independence and as an inevitable result have forgotten the sacredness of the feeling of participation in rituals reflecting the magic and theurgic power of a divine creative Act—each human being has to rediscover the potency of symbols and to seek for his or her *individual* Creation Myth.

What better symbols could be used than those of an astrology whose roots are nourished by the ever new experience of the Sky and the mind-awareness of the vastness of the universe that has recently been revealed to us? What more significant symbol of creative beginning could there be than the entrance of the *potentially* independent individual into the open world of the Earth's biosphere after the pre-human and pre-individual period of embryonic gestation?

Only as the newborn breathes in the air that serves as the link between all living organisms—plants and animals—and thus becomes a participant in the activity of the biosphere, can the individual man or woman be considered existing. Before the embryo's heart develops a regular and characteristic rhythm, the womb contains only an animal. At this moment of *quickening*, the animal becomes a human being. With the first breath, a new stage in the circulation of the blood and the cerebrospinal fluid is reached; the human being ceases to be *only* 'human', having acquired the *potentiality* of becoming an 'individual person'. As such a potential individual, the newborn is also potentially able, sooner or later, to enter upon the sacred Path of transformation. Only potentially, however. The vast majority of human beings in our present world have not yet truly and actually become *individualized*. They are human beings whose consciousness, feelings, and capacity for action are mainly controlled by the dictates of a particular culture and religion, and deeply influenced by a climatic and magnetic biospheric environment.

The astrological chart erected for the moment of the first breath in a particular locality on the surface of the globe is a symbol of what is potential for the newborn, thus of how he or she *can best actualize* what he or she is born *for*. What the person is born for is essentially to reach the status of 'being-an-individual', autonomous, centered in the consciousness of 'being-I', and at least relatively free from a condition of basic subservience to his or her culture and its paradigms. So considered the birth-chart is the 'Creation Myth' of the individuality-to-be. It is a sacred symbol. As the celestial entities indicated in this complex symbol (the birth-chart) keep moving in their ordered courses, the symbol becomes a ritual—a sacred performance.

To see one's life as a sacred performance—and every moment and experience in it as a significant phase of the process of actualization of the birth-potential prefigured in the exact moment and place of birth—is to live, not merely one's individual 'solar myth,' but also one's galactic myth. It can now be a galactic myth, because the consciousness of the vanguard of mankind has come to demand for its symbols a frame of reference more vast than the solar system. The Milky Way should be considered in this frame of reference, because it represents the next step in cosmic organization beyond the solar system.

It is true that astronomers are now linking several galaxies into a metagalactic system, and there may be other similar groupings. But we cannot experientially know whether we should think of them as parts of an Einsteinian 'finite universe' or as separate cosmic aggregations speeding through the infinity of space. Human consciousness can only significantly and practically evolve one step at a time. It can now pass from the level at which we can observe an all-powerful autocratic Sun surrounded by subservient dark planets, to that of galaxies which constitute vast organizations of radiant centers of light we call stars, each galaxy separated from the next by enormous distances.

Transpersonal astrology as I have formulated it deals with the symbolic passage of human consciousness from the level of the solar system (or heliocosm) to that of the galaxy considered as a vast Company of light-radiating Star-beings. Such a passage is a ritual drama in several Acts and many scenes. An individualized person today can consciously and significantly *live* such a drama, phase-by-phase, crisis-by-crisis. It is a modern Great Mystery. But this 'living-experiencing' cannot be described by the words or images of a mind still structured by the demands and wants of biological and strictly personal existence; it can only be evoked through the power of symbols. To give precise 'information' about the transphysical and transindividual type of experience would be only to force into a material mold symbolic pictures that have been impressed upon the mind in rare moments of *clairthinking*.* It would be to project the galaxy upon the cloud-covered surface of our planet.

---

*This coined term is used in the same context as one would use *clairvoyance* (clear-seeing) or *clairsentience* (clear-feeling) or *clairaudience* (clear-hearing) with a meta- or parapsychological implication, above or beyond the norm.

What *is* projected is only a symbol of the transcendent reality; but because it is a symbol does not mean that it is 'unreal'. Neither does it mean that because there is such a transcendent, light-radiating, galactic reality, we, as physical beings living on a dark planet, are unreal. Every level of consciousness and activity is as *real* as any other—for the beings operating at that level, either because they are born at that level or have temporarily chosen to operate there for some purpose, perhaps a purpose we human beings can never truly understand. We can only reduce to terms of our own level of consciousness, words, and imagery what the purified and calm region of our mind has *reflected*—reflected rather than organismically experienced.

The glory of the human state of existence is that it is able to reflect such images of a higher level of existence. All human beings have this ability, latently, but few have fully actualized it. Man has this ability because *Man represents a stage of transition between 'life' and 'light'*—between planets and stars. Man is planetary matter on its way to the stellar energy we call light. This way, once it is understood and followed in clear consciousness and deliberate will, is the transpersonal way—the truly 'human' way. What we usually think of as human is actually but 'pre-human'. Human nature, as we generally picture it, is animal nature experiencing the attraction of galactic being and as a result finding itself in the tragic situation of being—to use old religious terms—neither beast nor angel, but a battlefield on which the two levels of being interact, at times in bloody conflict, at others in the exhausted slumber of what we call social normality.

Only a relatively few individuals today can truly 'understand' what this condition of life means. Most others either sleep in dreamless slumber or dream symbolic pictures which elude their understanding because the partially remembered dream is almost unavoidably distorted by refraction through the water of the emotional or cultural mind. For this reason, the individual who deeply feels the compulsion to move to the higher level of consciousness needs various kinds of help *to remember*, not so much the dream-scenes as their essential *meaning*.

More important still than remembering our 'great dreams'—the vivid ones that seem suddenly to awaken us—is to understand *all* events, crises, and changes of consciousness and attitude of our life. This is necessary in order to discover and fully realize where we stand on the path of transformation, what phase of the process of trans-human metamorphosis we are now experiencing, whence we came and whither we are going. We can only gain such an understanding if we take the Yin approach to life; if we 'flow with' life and let it whisper to us words that may evoke in our stilled and serene consciousness images of the road we are following and of the Holy City ahead still obscured by the smog of our forever extended intellectual suburbs, their vacuous comforts and insane distractions from the one thing that counts: to walk on—our mind, will, and emotions focused upon the glowing tower we see dimly outlined in the distance.

Astrology can be of real assistance for those who seek such an understanding of the transpersonal way. But it has to be *an astrology that aims at the discovery of meaning*—meaning latent in the symbols the astrologer has taken out of the wondrous experience of night-skies as potential guides on the road to the stars. It is a difficult, often tragic road, from crisis to crisis. But for a conscious individual, nothing really is of any importance save to walk on it—deliberately, undeviatingly and with total faith.

These two fundamental approaches to astrology—reflecting as they do two equally basic ways of living, feeling, and thinking—can be considered complementary as well as opposite. Each of them, if lived exclusively and dogmatically, produces negative results. We can reach a state of consciousness in which they are seen as complementary aspects of the human potential; but for an individual to intellectually and emotionally assert that at this time of history and in our Western world they are equally valid in actual practice is usually to fail to correctly assess and understand the situation in which we are living. It is to give in emotionally to the now-fashionable trend, according to which "every teacher really says the same thing" or that "we are all one"—and this is on the principle that we are now in an age of synthesis.

Synthesis, I repeat, is not chaos. Synthesis refers to the seed condition, for in the seed the entire *potency* of a vegetable species is condensed. There is no synthesis in the humus to which decaying leaves add only chemicals. Synthesis does not imply non-differentiation. Synthesis reveals the perfect form, not formlessness.

Unfortunately, the hippie and post-hippie generations which used psychedelic substances to start within their psyches a process of relative *deconditioning* have been made to believe that deconditioning is a positive state, and that purposeless and directionless living is an ideal way. Deconditioning is a necessary phase at the beginning, or rather *before* the beginning, of the positive path of transformation, but it is a phase to be *passed through*, not to luxuriate in or wander in aimlessly. To sing out ecstatically, "We are all one. Every teaching leads to the same Truth (with a massive capital T!)" is meaningless as a basis for practical action and formed consciousness. Unity is a necessary *background* realization; the facts we must face are differentiation and individualization. The goal, harmony, is the *organization* of differences, *not* their negation.

For the same reason, the kind of life of which Gautama the Buddha spoke as "the Middle Way" is but too often sadly misunderstood to mean lack of commitment in any definite direction, thus an unpolarized state of being, neither hot nor cold, black or white, but instead a meandering through undefined expanses of formless and tepid greyness. The path of the Buddhist Arhat and Bodhisattva is anything but grey or unpolarized. One cannot walk in two directions at once. Unfortunately, 'consciousness' has been so extolled at the expense of 'activity' and function within a larger whole that a condition of unformed and uncentered passivity—a *negative* Yin state—is often presented as the only alternative to an overly forceful (and therefore equally negative) Yang state of aggressive behavior and/or egocentric, intellectual thinking.

To tread the Middle Way means to avoid extremes; and all extremes are, strictly speaking, 'negative' because they destroy the essence of the path one treads. Both ambitious over-activity (spiritually as well as socially) and mediumistically uncontrollable passivity and openness are negative states. The Buddha preached against the rigid, ascetic practices of some Yogis, but his Dharma (or way of life) was a way of most positive self-control with regard to food, sex, and bodily comfort. It was a way of *structured openness and strongly oriented practices.*

The practice of transpersonal astrology, like that of transformative living, should also combine structure and openness inasmuch as it should be based on cosmic principles of organization—organization in space (the study of formal arrangements) and organizations in time (the study of cycles and their phases). But the transpersonal approach is evidently not the only valid one. It is, in fact, an approach that probably befits only a relatively few people, if followed genuinely and without deviation, and if all its implications are consciously accepted. Above all, it has to be clearly understood, and in order to understand it clearly it has to be seen in a proper social perspective. The next chapter will attempt to provide some basis for such an understanding.

# 3

## FOUR LEVELS OF INTERPRETING HUMAN EXPERIENCES AND ASTROLOGICAL DATA

Signs and symbols are produced in order to answer human needs. But there are various kinds of needs. The psychologist Abraham Maslow spoke of a hierarchy of needs, some very basic and a manifestation of what in my book, *The Faith That Gives Meaning to Victory* (1942), I called 'man's common humanity', others less vital or crucial. In my recent book, *Beyond Individualism: The Psychology of Transformation**, I speak of a hierarchy of *functions* rather than of needs, for the basic fact is that human beings can operate at several levels of activity and in terms of a consciousness whose scope and power of mental association and abstraction increases at each successive level.

### Four Levels of Human Functioning

1. All human beings operate at the *biological level* as physical organisms, as bodies. They act and react in order to satisfy a few basic organic functions such as oxygenation through breathing, blood circulation, metabolic food-assimilation, adaptation to changing temperatures and existential situations, self-protection through a complex system of nerve impacts and transmission, and

---

*(Wheaton, Illinois: Quest Books, 1979).

self-reproduction through sex. Each of these fundamental functions has what we might call psychic overtimes manifesting as drives, emotions, and an overall sense of being a particular organism whose singular characteristics differentiate it from other human organisms.

Synthesizing, as it were, all basic biological needs is the need for security, not only as a particular person, but more deeply still as a member of the human species; for, at the biological level, the preservation and expansion of the species as a whole is actually of greater concern—unconscious though it may be—than the safety of any particular body belonging to that species. As in all animal species, the single organism (the specimen) is always expendable; what really counts is what might happen to the species. This is the real basis of our concern with what happens to babies, or even embryos, and the very deep unconscious foundation of mother-love—for the child symbolizes the perpetuation and future of the human species. Even in our period of complex and intellectual civilization, people go to great lengths to try to preserve the remaining specimens of an endangered species; and this concern is a faint reflection of what remains in the modern mind of the purely biological state of consciousness—a sense of biospheric guilt.

2. When, on the basis of the need for security, human beings find in themselves the urge to come together and unite their strength against inimical forces or animals—not merely according to biological descent (the family grouping), but beyond or outside of the deep organic and psychic bondage to such strictly biological types of relationships—the *sociocultural level* of functioning is reached. At that level, the human being is more than a biological organism—a 'body'—he or she becomes a 'person'. No human being should be called a person unless he or she has become a functional participant in a social collectivity. Social participation at the level of physical activity produces psychic overtones, which, being common to all the participants, are gradually and inevitably *organized* into a particular 'culture', or to use a modern American term, a 'way of life'. But a culture is really far more than a manner of living. Culture establishes itself within the collective

psyche of a community as a power that controls the basic emotional responses to everyday living and the collective mentality (primitive and instinctual or more formally developed as it may be) of all the human beings born with the social organism and subjected throughout their growth to the religious beliefs, taboos, and mental assumptions of the community or tribe.

3. Most human beings today are still *primarily* controlled by biological drives modified and particularized by sociocultural forces. These forces are related to a specific racial temperament and the environment in which ancestors gradually formed a culture and thus a collective character transmitted from generation to generation. Nevertheless, for at least two-and-a-half or three millennia, a powerful and relentless trend toward 'individualization' has developed, especially in the Western world since the Crusades, the beginning of Humanism and the European Renaissance. This trend has been given power by the development of the analytical and rational mind—since the 6th century B.C. in India with the Buddha, as well as in classical Greece—and the new, little understood yet deeply felt belief that every person has within himself the power to act, feel, and think as a unique *individual*. This individual, being symbolically considered in Christianity as a 'son of God' and in Greek philosophy as a 'rational' being, was thought therefore to be superior to all biological and social compulsions. The individual was indeed superior to, and essentially independent from, the whole earthly stage on which he came to play some kind of rather incomprehensible part. This playing of a part was often given the meaning of learning a series of lessons which apparently require being, as it were, thrown into "human nature"—a nature essentially alien to Man's immortal Soul.

The present result—perhaps an end result—of such a trend toward an even more accentuated type of individualization has been our individualistic American society in which the individual is officially glorified and theoretically given an absolute value as well as 'inalienable rights'—and very few duties, usually perfunctorily performed and in conditions which today often make their performance quite meaningless.

When a human being, having become a sociocultural person, is actually able to operate, (or at least consciously and emotionally *claims* to be able to operate as a truly autonomous individual regardless of sex, color, race, class, or religion), new needs take form in this individual's consciousness; and they have to be met. These needs are particular to each individual; yet, they take specific kinds of forms for various groups or classes of individuals. While all these individuals are trying in some manner to assert their individuality *within* the particular culture in which they were born and educated, they have also very often to go *against* the rules, taboos, and mental assumptions of that culture. Their needs thus create for them more or less acute problems which the social, cultural, and religious organizations based on the paradigms and taken-for-granted beliefs of the collective past may not be able to solve, just because these problems have an inherently antisocial and anticultural character.

Within these individuals (or individuals-in-the-making, rather), primordial biological drives and 'programmed' sociocultural attitudes are still operative, usually as a deep, partially unconscious, and unrecognized type of bondage to the all-human biological and the more specialized sociocultural or religious levels of existence. Conflicts thus arise, which are often highly destructive or at least confusing if not bewildering. To meet these conflicts in a state of greater awareness and understanding, and to provide valid answers to the problems inherent in the process of individualization, can be the task that a particular kind of astrology can perform. But such an astrology must be geared to the demands of individuals as they have to deal with the generic and collective factors within themselves as well as with the uncertainties of their relationships to other individuals. Such relationships always have a more or less insecure, uncertain, and ambiguous charactaer because they are no longer founded upon the solid basis of commonly accepted sociocultural responses, as they were at the sociocultural level. At the individual—or individualizing—level, they are instead subject to the vagaries of egocentric reactions and personal feelings.

The *individualistic* level of consciousness and activity is thus the third basic level at which human beings can operate. This level has also its own specific needs, the fulfillment of which requires the use of a new type of symbols—or a new type of *interpretation* of old biological imagery and cultural-religious myths.

4. On the foundation represented by the individual level, a fourth level is possible: the *transpersonal* level. And the word transpersonal, as I use it, does not merely refer to what is beyond the personal. It implies a 'descent' of power that meets, as it were, the aspirations or 'ascent' of the human person who, having concentrated a long series of efforts toward the goal of actually becoming a free and autonomous individual, eager to stress his or her uniqueness and originality, has found these efforts leading to serious crises of belief and identity. During such crises, many confusing experiences and perhaps unclear revelations may take place—new feelings the individual could not account for, new visions and yearnings to merge with some mysterious subliminal reality, a new sense of 'belonging', but not knowing really to what, and quite often hearing some strange internal voices.

All these largely unexplainable inner occurrences—most likely matching and often superseding outer shocks or psychosomatic illness—are expectable once the trend toward individualization and autonomy reaches an acute and perhaps dangerous state. As this happens, the experiencer may react emotionally and violently by rushing in the opposite direction, for instance longing for communal living and/or religious security—whether along the lines of ancestral patterns, or following some glamorous, exotic personage or tradition. Whatever the case, conflicts and uncertainties are hardly avoidable. Guidance is sought. The need for new symbols, for a new *mythos*, may become insistent.

Astrology can provide an answer to this need, just as it has proven able to meet the needs developing at the level of individualization. But in order to answer effectively and convincingly the needs of the new level of consciousness, a different type of approach to astrology is again necessary. A new light has to be thrown upon the old symbols derived from visible discs or dots of light in the sky. New ones have to take form to meet the demands of as yet unfamiliar crisis-situations—and modern astronomy has provided us with potentially usable and most significant foundations for the birth of a new astrological *mythos*. On these foundations, a transpersonal kind of astrology may be built, not actually to 'solve' personal problems, but to transcend them by illumining the process that produces them, and what is still more important, by suggesting how they can be *used* in terms of a new kind of purpose.

## A Multilevel Astrology

Having thus briefly outlined the character of four basic levels at which human beings can operate, I shall now try to explain how astrology can take a different form and quality at each of these levels, and how astrologers operating at each of these levels should deal with the main data provided by the cyclic interplay of celestial motions.

The evolution of human consciousness and activity through these levels, when seen from the point of view of the historical process of civilization, is a slow process. This evolution is actually synchronous with the progressive development of the means of observation used by astronomers in order to build an increasingly broad and inclusive picture of the universe. The more encompassing this picture becomes, the easier it is for human beings to ascend to higher levels of consciousness. Nevertheless, today, just as at any historical period, only a minority of people operate consciously at the higher levels. There are human beings whose consciousness is centered at each one of the four levels I have defined.

In the majority of cases, that level is, I repeat, the biological level modified by strongly differentiated cultural patterns; yet because of the revolutionary state of crisis in which humanity as a whole is now living, a great many human beings find themselves attempting to move from one level of consciousness, and often activity, to the next. A dynamic, yet highly confusing situation thus exists and it is one of the main causes of the growing popularity of astrology. To many people, astrology now appears as a significant and inspiring means of interpreting what is happening to them and predicting what can be expected to happen personally and/or collectively. Astrology is also welcome because it can foster a sense of ordered and purposeful change, as well as meaningful process.

When I speak of consciousness being 'centered' at one level or another, however, I do not mean that a particular person acts or reacts *only* in terms of the values and purposes characterizing that one level. A human being does not remain a monolithic entity once he or she is able to think, feel, and behave at the more-than-biological and instinctual level. For example, a person may be utterly devoted to a religious cause or national community which, under certain circumstances so little values biological existence that it demands of its followers or citizens that in wartime they die to uphold the collective ideal; yet this same person may pass much of his or her time worrying about food, sexual and health problems, etc. The most independent, rugged individual not only still has to satisfy at least the most basic of his biological needs, he also uses the language of his culture in order to formulate his own opinions and life-goals; and whether in a negative or positive, destructive or constructive sense, he can hardly avoid acting and reacting in terms of the values of his family or natal social environment.

Yet, while a person's consciousness and activities may, and usually do (especially today), operate at more than one level, we can still speak of one particular level at which his or her 'identity' is mainly established. Whether steadily and in terms of a true 'center' of consciousness or not, a person functions mainly according to the values and rhythms of one level or another. Consciously or unconsciously, he or she also expects *to be met* at that level.

If a person asks for knowledge or guidance, the asking is thus conditioned, or at least colored, by the level at which he or she mainly operates, or by a conscious or subconscious attempt to move to the next level by gaining a new perspective. To gain a new perspective means to look at life in general and at oneself specifically from a new 'place', in terms of a different frame of reference—thus from a new level of consciousness and understanding. During the transition from one level to another, since the consciousness is not yet firmly established at the new 'place' or level, the person tends to expect to be met at the level at which he or she has functioned in the past—or in some cases to receive a 'spiritual push' that will facilitate the change in level by giving him or her a 'feel,' an experience perhaps, of what the new level is.

Confronted by a client asking for guidance as well as increased self-knowledge, the astrologer should first of all try to intuitively 'sense' the level at which the client is centered, or the level to which he or she is attempting at the time to direct his or her attention—and *as a result* is experiencing inner conflicts or crises in interpersonal relationships. I say 'intuitively sense' because it is not possible to ascertain from the birth-chart alone the level at which a particular client is operating, especially at a particular time in his or her life. Any horoscope is susceptible of interpretation at all possible levels. It may be the chart of a cat or a horse, the incorporation of a business firm, or a horary inquiry. And a particular person, while born into a family or social situation conditioning his or her operating at a particular level, may pass through a more or less prolonged and/or successful process of transition leading from that level to a succeeding one (or ones). Often the kind and quality of problems or inner conflicts that bring the client to an astrologer for a consultation present to the astrologer extremely strong 'hints' from which he or she can deduce the level of the client's operation or the nature of the transition from level to level he or she is in the process of making.

Much depends upon, first, the astrologer's understanding of the archetypal pattern of levels in human development and of the transition-process leading from one level to the next—then, upon his or her ability to apply this more or less abstract understanding to particular circumstances and cases. Three types of study and mental training may facilitate this ability: (1) Studying the concept of 'levels' in terms of, both, the psychological development of individuals and the historical evolution of human societies [I have outlined this in my book, *Beyond*

*Individualism: The Psychology of Transformation,* and I will develop the concepts further with a specifically astrological focus in the present volume]; (2) studying the historical social, religious, and cultural patterns of collective human development underlying and conditioning the kind of life-patterns and problems human beings encounter today; and, (3) studying the detailed, year-by-year biographies of well-known people along with their birth-charts and astrological progressions and transits (subjects we will study in Chapter 8).

The first point I mention is, of course, basic. In connection with all three points, however, I should say that study and the capacity for application are two different things. The second point I mention is also crucial, for many counselors today (including psychologists) fail sufficiently to appreciate the interrelatedness between cultural and personal development, between individual life-situations and problems and the overall socio-religious and historical context in which they, both, become possible and seek resolution. Only a thorough understanding of overall human development, both individual and collective, can enable a counselor to put into a truly holistic frame of reference and therefore into a workable perspective, a particular situation in a client's life.

The third point I mention has the possibility of integrating for practice the preceding two, yet to my knowledge it is an approach to astrological study followed by only a very few students and teachers. In many of my other works I have presented examples of points I was making, yet I have only rarely encountered a student who followed up by investigating the life of the person in order to truly understand what I was saying. Especially in my book, *Person-Centered Astrology,* in the chapter, "Interpreting the Birth-Chart as a Whole," I presented an entire case-study of a young man's life along with an outline of the kind of approach I took to a consultation with him. Here again, hardly any readers or students with whom I have discussed the matter of chart-interpretation noticed what I had said or thought deeply about the matter to follow-up what I had written.

It would be impractical and not in accord with the purpose of this book to present detailed case-study examples here. Giving examples would not only unfeasibly increase the size of this book, but would perhaps lead to imitative, rigid and rule-following interpretations. This book is not a 'text book' with rules to memorize. It is rather an attempt to open up a new, multilevel dimension in the practice of astrology. If it leaves much to the intuition and imagination of the astrologer, it does so because these are the faculties which must be awakened and developed in astrologers if they are to practice effectively *and safely* the kind of multidimensional and—especially, as we see later on,—transpersonal approach I am presenting.

Astrology *can* offer significant answers to situations at each of the four levels I have outlined, or during the transition between these levels. But this does not mean that every astrologer—no more than every psychotherapist—can handle equally well the situation a particular client presents. An understanding of all I have mentioned above should at least be of great assistance in realizing the nature and implications of a situation and adapting the interpretation of astrological data in the client's birthchart to his or her level of consciousness.

## The Biological Level of Interpretation

The need for air to breathe, food, some kind of physical exercise or 'play', relative security from destruction by predators or natural forces (extreme cold or heat, storms, floods), and for the satisfaction of the sexual instinct guaranteeing the preservation of the species imperatively require satisfaction. Primitive men and women pass most of every day trying to satisfy their hunger and insure at least a degree of security and comfort for themselves and their immediate family. Directly or indirectly, even modern men and women are often mainly, and in many instances almost exclusively, occupied with the satisfaction of these essential needs, albeit in quite a different way from their primitive ancestors. The rhythms and demands of biology are the foundations of human existence, activity and consciousness; yet in order for human beings to operate at 'higher' levels, these needs have to be brought under control or temporarily curtailed. When attempts to control them are made—and even more, when their satisfaction is opposed for 'higher' purposes called *spiritual* (at whatever level of consciousness this ambiguous qualificative is interpreted)—tensions, perhaps illness, and collective as well as personal problems are produced. Solutions to such types of problems have often to be found at a strictly biological level. Medical care, diet, a different occupation or way of life, physical exercise, and/or other strictly biological changes—even if they require changes also at the family, social, or business levels—may be imperative.

In human beings living in a modern, individualistic society, however, biological problems are very often (perhaps in most cases) by-products of tensions, frustrations, and ineffective activity at super-biological levels. An exclusively and strictly biological situation is rarely found. But in ancient types of tribal societies, astrology was never called upon to solve the problems of human beings as individuals. Even when larger kingdoms were formed and a horoscope was cast for the king, what was considered was the beginning of the king's reign—his accession to the throne, a matter affecting the whole kingdom—rather than the birth-chart of the king *as a person*. Even if the king's character and what might be seen in his 'destiny' were studied, it was only to the extent that these factors affected his reign and the nature of his rule.

I have discussed elsewhere* in some detail the implications of the fact that the astrology of tribal societies was 'locality-centered'. Astrology then dealt with the visible motions of Sun, Moon, stars, and planets from east to west in a sky strictly contained within the circle of the local horizon. The Earth was considered flat and the sky an immense and mysterious dome over the horizon-bounded soil in which the tribe was almost ineradicably rooted. The three basic repetitive sky-experiences of human

---

*The Astrological Houses: The Spectrum of Individual Experience* (New York: Doubleday, 1972).

beings were the alternation of days and nights, the cycle of seasonal changes, and the puzzling monthly changes in the shape of the Moon. The Sun was the Light of the Day; the Moon, the Light of the Night. These two 'Lights' (only much later were the Sun and Moon spoken of as 'planets' by astrologers) were the foundation of a strictly biological type of astrology.

The motions of the Lights could not only be related to experienced changes on the Earth's surface—daily, monthly, and seasonal—they could also be defined and eventually plotted out and measured by the way they seemed to affect the rising and setting of the most brilliant stars—primarily what was called their 'heliacal rising', and also their visible culmination at the zenith at 'midnight'.

In other words, seasonal changes were seen to be related to the relationship between the disappearance after sunset and reappearance before sunrise of certain brilliant stars, owing to their conjunctions with the Sun. This most likely led to the idea of a *solar* zodiac, while the passage of the Moon during the night through distinctive patterns of stars defined a *lunar* zodiac. It is probable that the lunar zodiac came first, at a time or in regions where matriarchy was the prevailing basis for tribal organization. The solar zodiac eventually became the dominant factor, together with the patriarchal type of society. Patriarchy presumably imposed itself as a system of organization when agriculture had to become individualized and regulated, and the growth of neighboring tribes made a struggle for more 'living space' and warfare an apparent necessity of human life.

At the biological level of astrological interpretation, the Sun and the Moon respectively symbolize the principles of Fatherhood and Motherhood. In ancient astrology, the Sun-Moon and day-night polarities represented in the realm of the sky what the male-female polarity was on earth in all animal life. This was the age of 'vitalistic' religions, fertility-cults, and worship of the male and female sexual organs (phallus and yoni) as symbols of the dualistic power of life. Even in the traditional European astrology, the Sun in a birth-chart was also supposed to represent the father, while the Moon referred to the mother.

The polarity principle—which took the form of the dynamic and balanced interaction of Yin and Yang in Chinese culture—was also applied to the planets, literally the 'wandering stars'. Unlike the so-called 'fixed stars' which remained in the same positions in relation to one another, the planets' motions were, at first sight, quite mysterious considering their peculiar forward and backward character. Yet these motions were sooner or later analyzed and shown to have a regular, cyclic character.

The planets were also paired: Mars and Venus, Jupiter and Saturn. The first pair was closely related to the Sun-Moon polarity, in the sense that Mars and Venus were believed to represent the more material or organic aspect of the universal life-process symbolized by the two Lights. Mars, the red planet, was related to the energetic, piercing activity of the male principle—the impregnator, the peasant breaking the resistance of the soil with his plough so that seeds could be sown in the dark humus. Venus was considered the celestial agent active in all seed—in man, the testicles, and in woman the ovaries. The Martian male, once a father, became the Sun; the Venusian female, once a mother, the Moon. The female rhythm of menstruation had long before been related to the cycle of the waxing and waning Light of the night.

The pairing of Jupiter and Saturn interpreted at the biological level is also quite obvious, astrologically speaking. Whatever lives has to expand and contract alternately. On the one hand, food has to be assimilated in order to produce growth and to maintain the basic rhythm of metabolism—ingestion, assimilation, and evacuation of waste-products. On the other hand, any living organism has to have a *specific* (i.e., belonging to its species) shape and structure giving stability to its internal operations. What Jupiter expands, Saturn stabilizes. The two principles are inseparable, just as inseparable as the Sun and Moon or the Yin and Yang principles—though these pairs of symbols operate within different frames of reference.

The planet Mercury—swiftly moving back and forth (three times a year) and never far from the Sun—is, at the biological level, the capacity inherent in all living organisms to coordinate their various organic processses. It therefore symbolizes the three nervous systems of the human body: parasympathetic, sympathetic, and cerebrospinal.

Ancient astrology dealt with the two Lights as a strictly bipolar unit—a twofoldness of vital power—and five planets. The entire system was seen operating within the zodiacal whole, which represented that aspect of infinite Space (the whole Sky) having a definite and observable impact upon life on Earth. To have such an impact, however, zodiacal space had to be dynamized by the Lights and the planets. This is the basis of the now little-understood concept of 'planetary rulership' according to which each planet 'ruled' two zodiacal signs—the two Lights, I repeat, being considered two aspects of one reality.

☉ ☽
Leo-Cancer
Virgo ☿ Gemini
Libra ♀ Taurus
Scorpio ♂ Aries
Sagittarius ♃ Pisces
Capricorn ♄ Aquarius

It probably took many centuries before the system was definitely built, but its meaning is very clear, and the principle of it was presumably established in the days of Chaldean astrology. What the system means is that there are six basic sub-levels in the operations of life in the human body; and Hindu philosopher-seers defined six differentiations of one cosmic power.* The planets are listed in what later astronomers proved to be the correct order of distance from the Sun.

This system of rulership is self-contained and its symbolism perfectly consistent. It clearly shows that the solar system, when interpreted at the level of biology and also of culture, as we will soon see, ends with the orbit of

---

*Cf. T. Subba Row, "The Twelve Signs of the Zodiac" (in *A Collection of Esoteric Writings of Subba Row*—Bombay: 1917).

Saturn—which now seems to have been proved to be the limit of the power of solar emanation (the 'solar wind'). At the biological and strictly cultural levels, the trans-Saturnian planets—Uranus, Neptune, and Pluto—are not only not visible, but not even considered or postulated.

Nevertheless, while life in the Earth's biosphere operates according to relatively stable rhythms, thus in a state of 'homeostasis', it is also subject to sudden shocks and, from the biosphere's point of view, unexpectable changes. Thus, any consistent and seemingly 'closed' system of interpretation of life-cycles cannot account for *all* that occurs. One must assume the existence of *metabiological* forces and influences. This means that the power of zodiacal space can also be dynamized by factors other than Sun, Moon, and planets.

In the past, two kinds of factors were considered to transcend the regularity of planetary patterns. One type was represented by comets, eclipses, and all celestial phenomena which did not fit into the scheme of planetary motion and rulership. The other type referred to the assumed possibility of the larger stars themselves having an individualized influence *if* the Sun, Moon, and to a lesser extent the planets were in exact conjunction with them. It is probable, however, that this kind of 'fixed stars influence' should only be thought of at the sociocultural level of interpretation.

## The Sociocultural Level and the 'Person'

An organized culture develops on the foundation of biological facts and experiences. No culture ever ignores, or even basically challenges, the validity of biological drives or instinctual urges, for cultural values are overtones of biological rhythms. But in various circumstances and for various reasons, some of these overtones can become greatly emphasized. Just as the quality or timbre of an orchestral instrument depends on the relative intensities of the fundamental and the overtones that its tones contain, so cultures differ from each other according to the way in which they deal with biological factors and various modes of collective activity, and accentuate some at the expense of others. These cultural differences can be considered the results of genetic (racial) and environmental (climatic and magnetic) differences, but other factors transcending the physical and biological levels may also be at work.

Actually, when human beings come together and no longer act *exclusively* because they are in close and compulsive biological relationship with one another, but because they *consciously* participate in a set of activities recognized to be of value to all participants, and such activities establish a lasting bond among all participants, the beginning of culture has occurred. Any culture is based on a similarity of interests and feelings, and on the willingness to *associate* in the performance of a series of activities whose character becomes more and more clearly defined.

This process of association generates a sense of community, which develops as what I call a *collective psychism*. The terms psychism and psychic have unfortunately been used in a variety of ways. When I speak in this book of 'psychism', I am referring to a form of 'bonding' (or a principle of integration) operating at a level transcending, even if rooted in, biology.What we define as 'life-force' (or *prana*) at the biological level becomes 'collective psychism' at the sociocultural level—a very definite, concrete and powerful force in the experience of the men and women who participae in the day-by-day, year-by-year development of a well-established community.

This psychic force binds the participants through common reverence for what essentially are images, symbols, and myths to which rituals and festivals give a concrete and actional character. The basic factor in producing and maintaining such a communal psychism is religion, which literally 'binds back' human beings who might have developed separative tendencies that would break the strictly biological power of common parentage and genetic roots. Human beings eventually develop such separative tendencies and experience the process of individualization, but such a process can be constructive in an evolutionary sense only if the human being has first evolved an objective consciousness—a structured mind.

The development of mind at first requires not only a well-built language, but also a definite set of religious-cultural Images and symbols. The sociocultural condition of consciousness is the necessary embryonic stage through which human beings have to pass in order to reach the *mental* level at which autonomous and conscious individuals operate. Culture is the womb of individuality.

Thus, the collective psychism that acts as a subtle, non-physical 'cement' in building and maintaining any particular culture (or what can better be called a culture-whole*), is to be regarded as the matrix out of which an independent power of thinking—still a rare thing today!—emerges after a long process of gestation. A culture-whole is a psychic entity having a definite existence. It is at the level of psychism that a society, large community or nation is at the level of the physical activities of a number of people associated in interrelated, common activities.

At the sociocultural level, a human being becomes a *person*. He or she is no longer merely a biological organism. He or she is, at least to some extent, consciously participating in a process of interpersonal relationship adding a powerful new dimension to the consciousness. Sociocultural taboos are superimposed over biological instincts. New patterns of behavior and new forms of restraint take a binding character. Culture always seeks to control biology—and this is the well-known *leitmotiv* Freudian psychology has endlessly developed. Control develops conflict, and conflicts often lead to neurosis.

What we call 'character' can be regarded from this point of view as a stabilized form of neurosis; but it may be a very positive and forceful kind of stabilization to which psychologists give the name 'ego'. We should understand, however, that the term *'ego' refers to a functional type of activity rather than to a definite psychology entity*. The ego, at least at this sociocultural level, is a *function*. It is an answer to a definite and urgent *need* of the whole organism. It changes its character as the need changes.

---

*Cf. my book, *Culture, Crisis and Creativity* (Wheaton, Illinois: Quest Books, 1977).

## The Planets' Meanings at the Sociocultural Level

In an astrology which deals with the needs and problems of a 'person' belonging to and participating in a particular culture-whole, the ego is represented by Saturn and the Moon. Saturn symbolizes, in general, all forms of sociocultural restraint, taboos, and socio-political or ethical rules. All of these are archetypally represented by the Father-figure, the symbol of social authority.

It is true that at the *biological* level of interpretation, the Sun in a birth-chart represents the father, but only in the sense that the father's sperm is involved in the production of the physical organism. At the level of the *personal* development of a child, the father as a dominant figure in the home is represented by Saturn. At both levels, the mother is symbolized by the Moon. At the biological level, the Moon's function of adaptation to the needs of everyday living is at first almost entirely performed by the physical mother (or mother-surrogate) taking care of the needs of the child's body and of its developing nervous system and mind. The mother is also, at least in an archetypal sense, the intercessor between paternal authority (or the imperatives of society) and the biological instincts and desires of the child whose organism seeks to develop its various faculties without regard for what it finds in its immediate or social environment.

At the sociocultural level, the ego has two basic functions. The first is to provide some kind of *security* in the confusing, strange, and at times seemingly inimical world in which the child is living: this is the Saturnian aspect of the ego. The second and related function is to develop mechanisms of adjustment or adaptation able to increase comfort, produce a sense of well-being and happiness gradually assuming an increasingly psychological character (lunar function). Behind the ego, however, another factor is at work to which I shall refer in the next chapter when discussing the meaning of the ambiguous little word 'self'. This factor has at first a strictly organismic character. It refers to that mysterious power of life that makes a vast collection of cells and organs, a body—an organized, living whole, not only with a definite structure, but with a center to which sensations, feelings, thoughts, and all experiences are eventually referred.

At the strictly biological level, there is presumably no actual center to the consciousness. Animal and vegetable consciousness is diffused through the whole species and its myriad of specimens. It is not 'self-consciousness' because it does not have a truly *objective* character. The strictly biological type of human consciousness is also totally involved in the activity of the body. But as human beings begin to develop at a sociocultural level, through the use of a language giving an objective character to their actions and reactions, and as the motives and purposes for their interpersonal relationships assume stable forms endowed with collective and mentally formulated values, the diffuse instinctual sense of *organismic unity* acquires the character of a focalized feeling of *personal identity*.

This identity is most definitely and almost ineradicably associated with the name the child was given by the parents. That name not only identifies the person at a social level; it becomes the nucleus around which a psychic sense of 'being I, myself' crystallizes. This feeling of 'being I' is a psychic factor—in the sense in which I have defined the word psychism—because it is *defined* by the name in terms of the collective being of the tribe or community, its religion and culture; but it is also *rooted* in the primordial biological sense of organismic wholeness. Thus, it is both biological and sociocultural. The sociocultural aspect of this type of identity becomes further defined when the human being acquires a social profession—and being a housewife and/or mother is a social profession. This profession gives a still more precise character to what then becomes the person's social status. This social identity may then crystallize into what Carl Jung called the 'persona'.

At the sociocultural level of astrological interpretation, the biopsychic centralizing factor in the human being is represented by the Sun, which can thus be given a twofold meaning: it still represents the vital principle that animates and sustains the biological organism and its drives (what is usually called the 'vitality' of the person), but it also refers to a central factor which, in whatever capacity the person operates in his or her community, gives a basic though rather undefinable character to his or her capacity to operate in interpersonal and social situations. This is what is meant by 'personality', or charisma, when highly developed.

As the process of individualization begins, this power of personality undergoes a gradual transmutation. On the basis of an increasingly developed and differentiated mental function, what was at first merely social identity—a characteristic way of being oneself in terms of social activity—becomes an increasingly separate and autonomous individual 'I'. In our present individualistic society, a gradual transmutation of 'personality' into 'individuality' may *start* very early in a child's life, but what most people today call individuality is nothing but a personality based on an ego developed in response to, and therefore conditioned by, the pressures and impacts of a sociocultural environment. Personality always remains bound to the collective assumptions, traditions, and models of a culture. We can truly speak of individuality *only* when a person deliberately severs the myriads of psychic threads attaching him or her to a particular collectivity and culture, and emerges as an at least relatively independent, individual self.

Because in our society individuality has been given such an absolute value and prestige as a 'goal' which everyone should attempt to reach, the power which the culture-whole constantly exerts over the would-be individual is often not recognized. The psychic center in the person has been glorified by repeating that 'every man is a king'; but few truly realize that even the most ideal king—the most absolute monarch—is a product of the sociocultural level of existence. The king may, in principle, have absolute power over his subjects; he may theoretically 'own' the land and the people of his kingdom. But the master is bound to his slaves, without whom he would not be a master.

In classical astrology the Sun was said to symbolize the king, the supreme authority. But the Sun's meaning in a chart is considered to be determined by the zodiacal sign in which it is located, and the zodiac is a collective factor. It symbolizes human nature. Seen at the sociocultural level, a birth-chart gives us a picture of a particular way in which human nature operates in a specific instance within a particular culture-whole. The zodiac is the foundation of the chart; it represents twelve fundamental and characteristic ways in which the potential of activity and consciousness inherent in a human being living within a society can or is most likely to be actualized. The actualizing power is said to reside in the planets. Each planet refers to a particular function of human nature; and the genius of astrology is that its claims that every functional activity in a human being can be referred to ten basic planetary categories can be shown to have substantial validity. Most astrologers, however, are not aware of how significant such an implicit claim really is.

At this level, the Sun and the Moon are considered to be 'planets', no longer the two 'Lights' as they were at the biological level of interpretation. They nevertheless represent the most basic functions in human nature, because, in their original polarity, they symbolize the operation of the life-force, without which there could be no social and cultural activity, no consciousness, and no personality. The Sun represents the life-force as a unitary power, and the Moon distributes that power wherever the organism needs it.

In terms of the development of personality, the Sun symbolizes the desire to be an important and powerful unit in the community or nation—the will to achieve whatever is possible according to the life-circumstances and the culture. But at the social level, this solar will is still so conditioned by the images and ideals the particular culture has produced that one should not speak of an individualized will, if one uses language and ideas precisely. The individual factor is still mainly, if not totally, subservient to the collective way of life and its standardized goals—for instance, in the U.S. the goals of being liked by one's peers, of fitting in to a 'team', of being successful, wealthy, etc. The Moon at this level also has to be interpreted as the feelings produced by special types of interpersonal relationships, whether at home, in school or in the world of business or the arts. These feelings, in our present-day American society (in a collective sense), are very different from those possible for persons that lived in old Europe, in China, or in a primitive African tribe. But today we are all so eager to be individuals and feel our own feelings or think our 'own' thoughts, that we forget how dependent we still are upon collective ideals or even fashions—and there are fashions in feeling and thinking (even among Ph.D.'s and supposedly objective top scientists), as well as in clothing and entertainment.

The planets closest to the Earth—Venus and Mars—refer essentially to what is usually called the personal or emotional life. As I have so often pointed out, Venus does *not* refer only or even primarily to love and the arts. It refers to the *sense of value*. On the basis of our organismic temperament, our religious, ethical, and cultural training since birth—and our previous experiences once we have them stored in our memory—the Venusian function passes judgment on whatever changes take place in the field of our consciousness. Whether at the biological or the psychic levels, Venus gives a positive or negative value to what is confronting us or occurring within us: it is good for us or bad, beautiful or ugly, with pleasurable or painful implications. On the basis of this Venusian evaluation, Mars mobilizes biological, psychic-emotional, or even mental energy and releases this energy either to meet the new situation or to run away from it. The way this mobilization occurs is determined not only by the biological temperament of the organism, but by the character of the ego—that is, of the security-factor (Saturn) and the capacity for adaptation to everyday change (the Moon).

Jupiter performs a particularly significant role at the sociocultural level because it is essentially the symbol of 'social' activity. For an activity to be 'social', it must be based on the realization that in cooperation there is strength, and that only through interpersonal communication and communion of feelings and ideals can a human being actualize what is potential in *human* nature. Thus, Jupiter stands for good fellowship, and for all achievements that require collaboration on an organized scale and on the basis of the existence of a well-established sociocultural system—a culture-whole. The existence and maintenance of this culture-whole depends also on Venus, for it is the Venusian function that provides the great images, myths, and personal examples that are the 'soul' —the magnetic power and binding psychism of the culture. Thus at the sociocultural level, Jupiter and Venus are considered the most 'benefic' planets. They are benefic simply because they are responsible for what we consider most valuable and important at the level at which most people are still operating—and for no other reason.

The social function would lack a stable character and might run amok in an orgy of expansion if it were not balanced by a Saturnian sense of order and form. I have already spoken of Saturn as the drive for security, but there can be no personal security except where stable forms of order and organizational structures control the development of interpersonal, social or business relationships. A society needs laws and at least some kind of police force or collectively accepted authority, just as a human being needs a skeleton and plants need cellulose cell walls. Because there is, in most human beings, a centrifugal urge for self-assertion and often a deep restless feeling that change is essential for growth (a typically *human* characteristic which we will see associated with the symbol of Uranus) the Saturnian function is most often given a somber and binding character. Venus also, in a sense, binds; but its binding is in terms of values and apparently subjective psychological images which seem easily modifiable—though this is often an illusion. Saturn's binding has a very concrete, unyielding, often harsh character. So the planet is deemed to be 'malefic', though without its capacity to form stable and defendable boundaries, there could be no personality and, at least on this Earth, no realization of identity and selfhood: there can only be center where there is circumference. Problems develop when the organism-as-a-whole at the biological level, and the person at the sociocultural level find themselves in an environment which is so inimical and dangerous that the security drive dominates most aspects of living—or when an internal situation, e.g., an ill body or a weak person torn by inner conflicts, requires a rigid type of control of self-discipline.

Mercury, close to the Sun, refers on the one hand (biological level) to the most basic operations of the solar vital energy—that is, to the capacity of the organismic power of integration to manifest through currents of electrical nerve-energy—and on the other hand to the mental processes which are generated and, to a large extent, controlled by the Jupiterian organizational and administrative processes giving form, direction, and purpose to the functional (and in some cases, dysfunctional or criminal), operations of the members of the society as they relate to one another (sociocultural level). Saturnian factors also act upon the Mercury-mind, compelling it to follow definite, 'logical' and legalistic procedures—or at times to cleverly circumvent them, which is another way of being conditioned by them.

## Nodes, Eclipses and the Trans-Saturnian Planets

An added factor in the traditional and classical type of astrological interpretation at the sociocultural level are the Moon's Nodes. They are produced by the intersection of the planes of the Earth's and Moon's orbits. When two such planes intersect, a line of intersection is produced. In the case of the Earth and Moon, this line cuts the Earth's orbit (the ecliptic, which is also the tropical zodiac) at two points, the north and south nodes. Eclipses of the Sun and Moon can only occur when their mutual conjunctions occur close to the nodes in longitude.

Eclipses were once thought to be the portent of unexpectable, and thus more or less catastrophic (or at least upsetting) events. One of the Lights was being 'swallowed up' by a cosmic dragon—hence the north and south nodes have also been called the dragon's head and tail. When the two Lights are in exact alignment— which can only occur at a New or Full Moon near the nodes—a total eclipse takes place. If this happens at New Moon (soli-lunar conjunction), the Sun is eclipsed; at Full Moon (soli-lunar opposition), it is the Moon.

It would seem logical to say that when the Sun is totally eclipsed the Moon absorbs, as it were, all the solar power. What the Earth receives is only lunar power, and this condition is likely to influence whatever may develop during at least the fortnight between the New and Full Moon—and perhaps, it is often claimed, a much longer period. The Moon symbol in such a case is, as it were, glorified at the expense of what the Sun represents, and the Moon always basically refers to the past. Even though the Moon represents the capacity for adaptation, this capacity operates on the basis of the tradition or knowledge acquired in the past. A total solar eclipse may thus be considered a glorification of the past. A typical example is that of Mussolini, who proclaimed a new 'Roman Empire' in 1936 around the time a solar eclipse occurred near the position of the Sun in his birth-chart. An old image was revivified, but it nevertheless collapsed within a relatively few years.

On the other hand, at the time of a total lunar eclipse, the traditional perspective born of past experiences of adjusting to life and society is blotted out by an eagerness to meet experience in a new, original manner. When a solar eclipse occurs on a degree of the zodiac occupied by the Sun, Moon, a planet or angle in a person's birth-chart, or when such a degree and its opposite are involved in a lunar eclipse, whatever is on these degrees is likely to feel some effect. But the effects can be varied and often not clearly marked.

It is particularly important to stress that when dealing with the nodes both of them should always be considered, and not only the north node as is often done. We are dealing here with a *line*, not with mere *points*. Similarly, an astrologer should never consider the Ascendant of a birth-chart alone. The position of the Ascendant necessarily implies that of the Descendant on the opposite degree of the zodiac, because Ascendant and Descendant refer to the *line* of the horizon (in two-dimensional projection). The Midheaven and Nadir are also created by the meridian *axis* and should always be studied and evaluated together.

The other planets of the solar system also have nodes which establish relationships between their orbits and the orbit of the Earth. As I stated long ago in an article on 'orbital astrology' and in a chapter of my more recent book, *Person-Centered Astrology*,* such relationships

---

*"The Space Era and Orbital Astrology," HOROSCOPE Magazine: July, 1961.

between orbits have a non-personal, almost cosmic or 'fate-ful' meaning—for they deal with *space* and not with the planet as a *material mass.*

In the case of the Moon's nodes, we are dealing with what might be called the karmic way in which the Moon's function operates in a human being. But the word karma should not be used only in the sense of 'bad' karma. Karma simply refers to the fact that any new cycle of existence is always in some manner related to or is a sequence of a previous cycle. The new cycle inherits from the old some *unfinished business* which needs to be dealt with, but it also inherits the results of some achievements. More specifically, the Moon's north node symbolizes new possibilities of growth on the basis of what has been accomplished 'in the past'—let us say, in 'past incarnations', although the concept of reincarnation is most ambiguous, or at least far more complex than popularly interpreted. On the other hand, the Moon's south node indicates in symbolic terms the pitfalls that the inertia of the past (or subconscious memory of past failures), places in the way of personal fulfillment. We should not forget that a person is *first of all* operating in a biosphere with a long evolutionary past and in a society and culture conditioned equally by ancient, collective failures as well as great achievements. Thus karma is *never* to be considered solely a personal matter; for it is also produced by a collective situation inherited from a long series of past generations.

The Moon's nodes have a retrograde motion in the zodiac, and the nodal axis completes one cycle of the ecliptic in about 18⅔ years. The nodes of the planets are also moving, apparently in direct motion, at various but much slower speeds, most of them less than one degree of the zodiac per year.

Unfortunately, what I consider a basic misconception regarding planetary nodes has recently been introduced into astrological interpretation. At least some astrologers treat them as if they were observable entities like planets. Yet, I repeat, the nodes refer solely to the intersection of orbital planes, and such intersections are neither directly

---

*Person-Centered Astrology,* Chapter 5. "Planetary and Lunary Nodes" (New York: A.S.I. Publishers, 1976).

observable nor entities. They are truly metaphysical factors—factors to be calculated by the mind—which deal with space, orbital space.* There is obviously some difference between the calculation of lunar and planetary nodes, because the Moon revolves around the Earth, while the planets revolve around the Sun. The basic frame of reference in relation to nodes, however, is neither the Earth nor the Sun, but *the Earth's orbit*. The only thing that should be considered is where the orbit of any other celestial object intersects the Earth's orbit. This would be the case if we dealt with the intersection of the galactic plane or any other plane of cyclic motion and the Earth's orbit.

In the great majority of cases, planetary nodes are of no real meaning in the lives of human beings. They acquire at least potential meaning when a person, as a participant in a sociocultural whole, can be considered a mouthpiece or channel for the operation of collective forces. If the person has reached the stage of individual development at which he or she is actually conscious of what happens through his or her being, then the transpersonal level has been reached; but if there is no consciousness of being an agent of some supersocial and supercultural Power, but only a kind of *unconscious mediumship*, the person still operates at the sociocultural level.

At that level, the trans-Saturnian planets—Uranus, Neptune and Pluto—also act mainly in an indirect and collective manner; that is to say, they operate through changes occurring in the society or cultural as a whole— for instance, as changes in life-style, fashion, and education, or changes in the political and economic structure of a nation. To the great majority of people living

---

*Nodes are 'exact points' only in an abstract sense. At such points there is actually nothing. They exist only by *isolating on paper* two orbits and calculating where they intersect. In fact both orbits are parts of much larger orbits, and as every celestial body moves at terrific speed one cannot speak of nodes as actual entities. This is why the *mean position* of any periodically moving factor is more valid an element in the language of astrology than a so-called 'actual position.' All planetary longitudes used in astrology refer to the *centers* of celestial bodies, thus to the motions of abstract points.

in more or less normal and relatively stable periods of cultural and political evolution, such changes cause a minimum of personal problems; people readily adjust to them. Yet, since the process of individualization has reached a stage at which it has become a public issue, and the attainment of a state of conscious, free and autonomous individuality is presented in one form or another all over the globe as the ideal goal of human evolution, the trans-Saturnian planets play a critical role even at the sociocultural level of astrological interpretation.

When in a birth-chart either Uranus, Neptune or Pluto is conjunct, opposed or even square a planet, or is found at the horizon or meridian, whatever function or mode of personal expression is involved, tends to take a non-traditional or unusual form. This function often becomes a source of irritation or dissatisfaction, but in some instances, the person, through an exaggeration or extraordinary development of the function, may gain fame or notoriety.

In the following chapter we shall see how each of these three planets tends to operate during the process of individualization. However, the astrologer should realize that most people today believe they are already at a far advanced stage of this process. This may not be the case, and it is better in principle not to assume that any client has to be treated as an individual whose problems have a character transcending the sociocultural level. Yet, because our entire society is in a crisis of transformation, facing the critical necessity and potential of taking a radical step in its evolution, most of the people who are 'progressive' enough—or sufficiently disturbed, restless, and confused—to seek astrological guidance can be considered to be at a stage of psychological development (and of relative alienation from the norm of the collective psychism of their sociocultural environment) which allows for the direct and cathartic impact of Uranus, Neptune, and Pluto.

Such persons also may have failed to adapt to some basic transformation, either in their biological environment or diet, or else in the ancestral way of life they had so long been taught to accept unquestioningly as the one and only good and valid type of existence. In all such instances, Uranus deals with upheavals that challenge the worth and meaning of the great images of the sociocultural tradition; Neptune tends to dissolve encrusted prejudices, sap the strength of all that the Saturnian drive to security has built and the Jupiterian ideals had presented as desirable achievements. Pluto adds a note of extremism or fanaticism to any crisis or religious, political, or artistic 'conversion'. It tends to make any transformation irrevocable and to destroy any safe means of retreat. Pluto atomizes all that has solid substance, reducing every concept or feeling-experience to its barest essentials—and such a process of 'reduction' can lead the mind to a state in which everything appears to be inherently absurd and utterly hollow. Nevertheless, it is a state of chaos out of which a new world may be born.

This 'new world' need not be really or radically new. It may be built out of fear of the unknown and constitute only a resurgence of ghosts acquiring at least a temporary substantiality. Neptunian crises may lead to a psychological 'return to the Mother'—a largely unconscious sinking into the collective psychism of a revived allegiance to some old or exotic but traditional way of life. Plutonian crises, on the other hand, often lead to totalitarianism or gangsterism—a resurgence of dependence upon a father-image or ruthless authority with a strictly personal or ideological character.

It is in this sense that the three trans-Saturnian planets, which are the most usual symbols of transformation, can operate in the lives of people who are still basically acting, feeling, and thinking at the sociocultural level. Yet the 'spirit of the time' is relentlessly pushing toward a truly new state of human existence, a state in which society and all collective factors are meant to be only instruments making it possible for human beings to take as their most fundamental and valuable goal *fulfillment as individuals.*

# 4

# THE INDIVIDUAL LEVEL
# OF INTERPRETATION

## The Mandala Symbol in Astrology

Briefly recapitulating the preceding: The activity of any living organism operating at strictly the biological level—whether an animal, a plant, or a human being—is controlled by a power that resides in the species, not in any one of its particular specimens. This power is able adequately to meet the conditions of life in the environment, to protect, maintain, and, if possible, expand the role the species plays in the biosphere, each life-species having a particular function to perform within the extremely complex pattern of biospheric inter-depend ence.

When a human being operates at the strictly biological level, he or she, like any animal, is controlled by this generic power operating in the form of instincts, and his or her consciousness has a compulsive and organismic character. It is probably also diffuse and subjective, for it is neither objective nor 'reflective' or self-conscious. It may be compared to the rather unformulatable feeling of health experienced by a young person who has never experienced illness, directly or vicariously.

At the sociocultural level, a human being participates as a 'person' in the limited and structured field of activity of the society in which he or she was born and educated. The mind of this person is given a characteristic form by a particular language and by collective patterns of beliefs and assumptions impressed since birth upon his or her developing psychism. The validity of these patterns is unquestioned. In primitive societies or archaic kingdoms, a person is almost totally identified by the clan, class, or religious group to which he or she belongs. The person has a role to play and a name which represents that role. If the person conforms to the role and to what society expects or demands, he or she is secure within the limits of the birth-status. Thus, a sociocultural and ethical level is added to the biological level; and the demands of the two levels at times clash, causing more or less serious disturbances.

If a normal, well-adjusted person, operating at the sociocultural level and relating to other persons according to definite social and ethical patterns of relationships, experiences conflicts between biological urges or attachments and the social patterns which condition and often rigidly rule his or her life, religion is there to help re-establish some kind of relatively harmonious adjustment. In such a person, the feeling-experience of 'being I' exists and may play a very important role; but it is based on all that refers to the *place* (position or status) the person occupies in a family and in the larger field of society. This feeling-realization of 'being I myself' is almost ineradicably associated with a name. The person asked who he is will say: I am Peter Smith, and usually adds what his family status, occupation, or profession is. These names and labels characterize the ego-sense of identity.

Looking from an astrological point of view at the situation of a person identified with a sociocultural situation, such a person's ego is (as already stated) symbolized by Saturn and the Moon: Saturn refers to the social status or position which guarantees social security as well as biological livelihood, and the Moon to the capacity to adjust one's feelings and reactions to what this status or position requires. At that sociocultural level, a person's birth-chart is like a map showing the special character and intensity of the basic natural factors operating within this person and the particular manner in which they are interrelated (astrological aspects). Yet such a chart has, however, no *actually individualized and autonomous center*. The ego does not constitute such a center. It oscillates and is swayed by forces over which it has no steady control. It is only the *center of gravity* of an ever-changing situation.

It is *only* when the process of individualization has begun, and an individualized consciousness based on a deep, often poignant feeling of separateness and estrangement or even alienation from the level of strictly social activities and relationships has asserted itself (at least partially and sporadically), that one can speak of the existence of a truly individual center. In a birth-chart that center is found where the horizon and meridian intersect. It is there that the individual center—the real 'I' disengaged from family, social, and eventually, cultural patterns—is to be found. It is there as a potential and gradually actualizable center. Such an individualized birth-chart can then, but *only then* be interpreted as a *mandala*.

A mandala, in the usual two-dimensional sense of the term, is a configuration revealing a more or less symmetrical arrangement of various kinds of forms, scenes, and symbolic images around a center. Usually the mandala has an overall circular form and, in the majority of cases, a basic quadrangular structure is apparent. Tibetan mandalas are particularly well-known, and they are used in meditation to focus the mind and to reveal through symbolic senses, pictures, or diagrams the nature of a process of integration leading to a vivid experience of a central Being or quality of being. In European Gothic cathedrals, rose windows are also considered to be mandalas. In them we may see Christ as a central figure surrounded by his twelve disciples. In classical astrology, the zodiac is also often represented as a mandala, with the Sun at its center. A human body may also be pictured surrounded by the twelve symbols of the zodiacal signs or constellations.

At the individual stage of human existence, the birth-chart represents *the mandala of personality*. Its center symbolizes the mysterious power and experienced feeling to which the little word 'I' refers. At the level of an individualized human consciousness, this 'I' should no longer be considered an ego in the sociocultural and Saturn-Moon sense of the term, though it will try *to use the* types of functional activity symbolized by Saturn and the Moon for its own purpose. How then can we speak of this profound realization emerging in a human being who feels himself or herself 'separate' from the family and culture that produced the material body, emotional temperament, and mental structure that altogether constitute his or her personality?

Most people would refer to this realization of being an autonomous and essentially (if not actually) 'free' individual as the manifestation of a *self* that has at last succeeded in becoming aware of its own existence as an independent entity. This word 'self' has, unfortunately, been used in many ways and in reference to many levels of consciousness and activity; its use, whether or not one capitalizes the first letter of the word, can be extremely confusing.

In my main philosophical work, *The Planetarization of Consciousness,* * I stated that one has to postulate in every structured and organized system of activity and consciousness—every living whole of existence—the active presence of a Principle of Wholeness. While we may speak of it in an abstract sense as a 'Principle', it has also to be considered a power of integration, a binding force. I spoke of it either as ONE or SELF. It is not, however, *a* one or *the* One. It has no particular form or attribute in itself. It simply *is* wherever an existential whole (an entity) operates. It inheres in *any* entity, be it an atom, a cell, a human being or galaxy. Without it there could only be an undifferentiated, diffuse, and infinite expanse of 'substance-energy', or—in a purely abstract and transcendent sense—Space.

The seers-philosophers of old India have given various names to this Principle. When considered as a 'Presence' (an unsubstantial 'breath') within a human being, they spoke of it as *atman*. In relation to the whole universe, they usually gave it the name *brahman*. The great revelation that took form in the ancient Upanishads was that atman and brahman were essentially identical. The

---

*Now in its fourth edition (A. S. I. Publications, New York: 1977).

same power of integration, the same mysterious, actually unreachable and ineffable Presence, was inherent in all living beings; and as life itself was but one of its particular modes of operation, the whole universe and all it contains were alive.

As a Principle and power of integration SELF is present everywhere, but its mode of operation differs at each level of existence. Since a human being functions and is conscious at several levels, SELF has to be understood in a human being in several ways—biologically, socioculturally, individually, and eventually, transindividually. It is best, however, not to speak of a 'biological self' or an 'individual self', but instead of a biological, sociocultural, and individual *state of selfhood*. Biological selfhood has a generic and, in the usual sense of the term, unconscious character; sociocultural selfhood has a collective character; and individual selfhood is achieved by undergoing a long and arduous process of individualization. The process of human evolution has so far consisted in bringing the *sense of self* from the unconscious darkness of the biological nature to a condition of ever clearer and inclusive consciousness through the development of ever finer, more complex cultures and of ever more responsive and conscious individuals. A still more inclusive and universal realization of SELF should be achieved when the state beyond individual consciousness is reached—what I have called the Pleroma state of consciousness.

Because the process of individualization of human beings began many centuries ago and was given a definite and objective form through the development of an abstract and intellectual kind of mind, the great religions and philosophies of the last millennia have in various ways stressed the importance of the individual stage of selfhood. Because of the crucial importance of the Hebraic tradition and its basic concepts in our Western civilization, I might mention here the rather ambiguous, yet in a sense revelatory manner in which the ideal of individual selfhood was apparently presented to the consciousness of the founders of that tradition.

In the Bible (Exodus 3:14) what is usually translated as "I Am That I Am" (*Ehyeh Asher Ehyeh* in the Hebrew) is revealed to Moses as the new Name of God, superseding, as it were, earlier ones which may have referred more specifically to the power of 'life' (biological level). In the following verse God moreover refers to himself for the first time as JHVH (Yod-He-Vau-He), the sacred word often spoken of as the Tetragrammaton. I believe that this Name was revealed to Moses because he was the leader of a most likely quite heterogeneous group of tribes, and his task was to integrate them into one 'People' under a definite kind of structural Law which later became the Torah.

The foundation of the Tetragrammaton comes from the same Hebrew root (hayah) as Ehyeh, 'to be'. Although Ehyeh Asher Ehyeh has almost universally been translated as I Am That I Am, etymologically and more precisely, it gives expression to something more like 'I will be what I will be'—or even 'I will be what I am becoming' —for the fact is that the modern Hebrew language has no word for simply "I am." The exact meaning of the Biblical statement is indeed a matter of great controversy among the Rabbis, ancient or modern. The original Hebrew meaning at any rate seems to indicate a fourfold process of integration rather than an established fact. It should be considered a mantram; and it may have been meant to apply to not only the integration of tribal groups that had separated themselves from the biological realm which Egypt came to symbolize in the Hebrew tradition, but at least eventually to the individualization of human consciousness and will in any person ready to pass through a long period of spiritual gestation—the long, difficult, and often tragic process symbolized by the forty years of wandering in the desert.

In the Kabbalah—the esoteric Hebrew tradition—it is said that "Man is still in the making." Man, as an individual, is even today in the making. The process of individualization began in earnest and in a public sense around 600 B.C.—a period marking a definite turning point in the evolution of the consciousness of Man as an archetypal being. It was the time in which lived Gautama the Buddha in India and Pythagoras in the Greek world; and their respective teachings opened the way to the slow and gradual actualization of a new mode of consciousness and mental developmeńt necessary for the process of individualization. From this time on, it became *possible* for all human beings to steadily experience the feeling of 'being I' in a truly individualized, stable, and centralized manner; but though this possibility began to impress itself upon social ideals and (with Christianity) religious institutions, only a relatively few human beings have been able fully to actualize the new potentiality. This, I must add, apparently always happens when a new opening in consciousness is made, so great is man's resistance to change at both the biological and the sociocultural levels.

The basic purpose of a mandala, especially in Asia, is to evoke, through powerful symbols, various aspects or stages of the process of consciousness integration and centralization. By meditating on a mandala, which in most cases has a basic fourfold structure, the individual-in-the-making is at least theoretically helped to actualize in a correct and meaningful manner the innate potential of his or her particular nature. On this Earth plane, the number 4 is a basic key to the process of concretization of what at first is only an ideal or potentiality. In Carl Jung's psychology, the mandala-concept is stressed because according to this great Swiss psychologist the field of consciousness has a center, and consciousness operates in four characteristic ways which he called 'psychological functions': sensation, feeling, intuition, and thinking.*

An astrological birth-chart can be regarded as a mandala if it is understood to be a symbolic two-dimensional representation of a centralized field, not only of consciousness, but of purposeful activity. This field—the field of space surrounding the newborn—is primarily divided into four areas by the horizon and the meridian lines forming a perfect cross. The four points at which the cross meets the circumference of the field are called the Angles. On the horizontal line, they are the Ascendant (or eastern point), and the Descendant (or western point), and on the

---

*Cf. Carl Jung, *Psychological Types.* See also my book, *The Astrology of Personality,* "The Dia! of Houses", p. 210ff, where I relate these Jungian categories to the Angels of the birth-chart.

vertical line of the meridian, the Nadir (or Immum Coeli) and the Zenith (or Mid-Heaven). These four angles represent the four characteristic types of activity which participate in the building and development of a conscious and stable center within the whole human being. They are the 'roots' of the individualized consciousness.

Through these roots the I-center can draw sustenance and power from the world of biological experiences and the realm of sociocultural cooperative activity and interpersonal relationships. It can also receive what may become actual 'Illumination' from the eastern angle, the Ascendant; for it is at this symbolic point of sunrise that the 'I' can most effectively discover its purpose—or rather the purpose of the birth of a living organism that served as the biological foundation for the rise of a particular form of consciousness to the level of a stable and operative individuality.

This biological foundation is symbolized in the birth-chart by the Nadir or I.C. At the sociocultural level, whatever guarantees a relative degree of permanence and psychic security (particularly the home and the land of birth) is represented by this angle. It is where an individual can find the particular quality of his or her rootedness in the culture which formed his or her concrete personality.

The western angle (the Descendant) refers to the power that, in the process of individualization, the consciousness draws from the relationships which both the physical organism (the body) and the socializing person constantly enter into in everyday living. No human being is born or lives in a vacuum. Living is relating—whether the relationship is given the positive meaning of steady and fruitful partnership in personal love and social cooperation or the negative meaning of enmity. Consciousness grows out of relatedness. Through the experience of close relationship (whether positive or negative), the I-center becomes more clearly able to define the quality of its being and the scope of its constructive activities.

The fourth angle is the Zenith (or in terms of zodiacal longitude the Mid-Heaven), and it symbolizes the power the individualized consciousness draws from participation in any larger organized system in which it plays a definite role. At the sociocultural level, this angle refers to professional activity, but more generally to whatever brings the I-center in touch with a broader, more encompassing system of being.

Every organized system of activity and consciousness, while it is a whole having component parts, is also a part within a greater whole. The universe is a hierarchy of wholes, and consciousness inheres in every whole. But there are levels upon levels of wholeness. In every whole there is a point (or rather an area of potential activity) at which the lesser whole can contact and receive some influence, power, or 'blessing' from the next greater whole. This point is symbolized in astrology by the Zenith. For the person who is striving to become individualized and to reach fulfillment as an individual, the next greater whole in whose being he or she can *actually* participate may only be his or her community, nation, or culture. It should eventually be Humanity-as-a-whole—and by Humanity I mean far more than a chaotic collection of human beings spread around the globe; I mean a vast planetary Being that is also in the process of unfolding Its immense potential of activity and consciousness.

While at the Nadir an individualized human being is still able to find a power of sustainment in the energies of the biological functions and in the cultural tradition, at the Zenith the individualized being should eventually open himself or herself to the *descent* of a 'transindividual' power and to the revelation of the place and function he or she *potentially* occupies within the vaster whole of Humanity. What could only be 'intuitively' sensed as the uniqueness and strictly individual purpose of life at the Ascendant (the symbolic sunrise point) can in principle be clearly seen and concretely applied at the Zenith (the symbolic noon point). At the Zenith, when the individual is ready to take this radical step, he or she may be 'reborn' as a full-fledged and, in a real sense, *consecrated* individual, able, egolessly and consciously to act as an agent of Humanity. Such an individual can then be empowered by Humanity (then perceived as a spiritual organism of unanimous consciousness—a Pleroma of transindividual beings), to actually perform what he or she was born *for*, his or her *dharma*. The *astrological symbol* of this empowerment, and of the Source of the power made available to the individual for the welfare of the whole, is a star in the vast system of organization we call the Milky Way, the galaxy within which the solar system and all it contains constitutes but a small unit.*

In every human being, the potentiality of eventually becoming related to such a 'star' is inherent; but it is only a potential, a very distant one in most instances. In order to actualize this potentiality, a human being has, step by step, to raise the level of his or her consciousness from the biological to the sociocultural, then to the individual level —and not merely his or her consciousness, but also the quality and character of his or her activity. The process leading from the biological to the sociocultural level can be called the process of *enculturation;* from the cultural to the individual, it is the process of *individualization.* The path that leads beyond the individual is the *transpersonal* Path; and I shall devote the next chapter to it. I shall try to suggest how to approach a type of astrological interpre-

---

*The Zenith and Mid-Heaven (and Nadir and Immum Coeli) technically and astronomically are related to two different frames of reference. Zenith and Nadir refer respectively to two points of the sky, the former directly overhead, and the latter its exact opposite. If a person stands upright on the surface of the globe, the prolongation of his or her spinal column would be, above, one of the trillions of stars in the visible sky, and below, first, the Earth's center, then a point at the antipodes, then an invisible star above the other side of the Earth. The meaning of the Nadir and of the symbolic fourth House it begins is to be deduced, first, from the concept of the soil on which the person stands, then the Earth-center (the center of the planetary whole), then the realization that any existent is polarized by its opposite— objectivity (the visible sky) by subjectivity (the invisible inner center), light by darkness, etc.

In traditional astrology the terms Zenith and Mid-Heaven are usually used interchangeably. The Mid-Heaven is, however, astro-nomically a point in the zodiacal circle. It is still the point *above,* but classical astrology uses the zodiac as the foundation of all essential astrological meaning—although parallels of declination are also used which do not refer to the zodiac. When I have spoken of the star above the head, it is of course the star at the *actual* zenith. The Mid-Heaven is the *symbolical* zenith in any system based on the zodiac.

For a full discussion of stars, see my book *The Sun is Also A Star (The Galactic Dimension of Astrology),* especially Chapter 9., "The Challenge of Galacticity in Humanistic Astrology," p. 173ff.

tation meeting the most significant needs of individuals seeking to tread that path of radical transformation, or even only to orient themselves toward the distant goal that the concept of the transpersonal path may evoke in them once they have become dissatisfied with both the patterns of our society and the narrow, so often blind and aimless pseudo-individualism of 'doing my own thing'.

## The Birth Chart and the Planets in a Mandala-Type of Interpretation

Whether or not they clearly realize it to be fact, the majority of human beings, especially in the Western world, are struggling through the slow and arduous process of individualization. In interpreting the birth-charts of these individuals-in-the-making, it is therefore advisable and often imperative to assume that at the symbolic center of the birth-chart a centralizing entity—or power of integration—at least partially, perhaps weakly or spasmodically, operates. The birth-chart can therefore be considered a mandala; and all mandalas have to have a center and a circumference. Everything that is contained within this circumference should sooner or later be referred to the center. All the contents of the mandala of personality acquire their meaning by being related to the center. They are potentially, if not actually, powers which the central 'I' should be able to use in order to express itself, to establish its position and status in the social environment, and to leave a characteristic mark—the signature of its individual being—upon whatever it is able to affect.

Any integrative process requires some kind of boundaries which set limits to it and define its scope in spatial terms. When a birth-chart is considered a mandala, its center is, I repeat, the point at which the horizon and meridian axes cross. There stands, if not the actual individual, at least the potentiality of individualization—the individual-in-the-making. The circumference which sets limits to the field of existence of an individual—his or her basic living space—is, in present-day astrology, the

85

zodiac. The zodiac also symbolizes for the individual generic 'human nature', which also sets limits to individual development, yet not impassable ones. In the Western world, all but a few astrologers use what is called the tropical zodiac, which, to an astronomer, is the ecliptic, the Earth's orbit.

At the *biological level* of interpretation, the zodiac is the field of electromagnetic energy surrounding the Earth. As the Sun's rays strike our biosphere at constantly changing angles month after month, they release into it and induce varying types of energies. The twelve signs of the zodiac represent twelve fundamental types of energies. The day of the year a person is born determines the type of energy providing the foundation on which the different biological processes operate, each in its own organic manner. This solar energy is then distributed by the Moon, and modified by the functional use the planets make of it.

At the *sociocultural level*, a person's 'sun-sign' (the position of the Sun at birth in one of the twelve zodiacal signs), gives the astrologer some basic information concerning the 'character' (or 'personality' factor), of that person as he or she participates in family or social activities. By character is meant—or should be meant—the way of least resistance and maximum effectiveness this member of a society has found to operate among other members and in relation to a central collective authority. We have already seen what the other planets represent at this level.

When a birth-chart is interpreted at the *individual level*, the Sun symbolizes the 'will' of the individual. But it should be clear that such an interpretation does *not* invalidate the biological and the social meanings of the Sun in this individual's life. The power of will which emanates from the individualized Sun is *conditioned* by the organic vitality and the psychic state and character of the person, as he or she strives to establish a stable, steady, and powerful life-stance. What is called 'will' is the power of the I-center to order the mobilization of the biological and social energies operating within the circular space symbolizing the whole person in order to act in an individual way—thus to express its relatively unique character and purpose in life.

In modern astrology, the Sun is spoken of as 'planet', and so is the Moon. Yet neither the Sun nor the Moon is in fact a planet in an astronomical sense. In an individualistically oriented astrology, they are considered planets because they represent functions or powers which, at least theoretically, are at the disposal of the central being, I-myself—just as are the functions represented by the actual planets. Every planet and every astrological factor found within the birth-chart—the mandala of personality—must be referred to the I-center, which gives them a conscious and individualized meaning.

In an individualized person, biological vitality becomes will, and the collective psychism of the community, class, or nation takes a particular form symbolized by the Moon. We refer to this particular form when we speak of the 'feelings' or psychic state of a would-be individual as he or she struggles through the process of severance and detachment from the collective psychism in an attempt to experience 'rebirth' as a liberated, autonomous, self-actualizing individual.

Today the term 'psychic' most of the time designates phenomena and states of awareness which are outside of the field of what our particular culture-whole acknowledges as reality, yet which somehow are able to affect those participating in that field. I believe that many, if not most of such psychic phenomena have their roots in the disassociation occurring in a person's field of consciousness when he or she is pressured by special life-circumstances to sever the threads of attachment which link his or her 'inner life' to the collective psychism of family and/or culture. The pressure may also be exerted by some transcendent power or group-entity constituting a sort of whirlpool of consciousness within the collective psychism of the culture—somewhat in the sense in which psychological experiences that have been repressed by the ego (for reasons of security, or out of sheer inertia and perhaps fear) tend to aggregate as 'complexes'. These complexes seek self-expression, or even revenge, by pressing upon and perhaps overwhelming the defenses of the ego.

In other cases, however, these extra-conscious pressuring factors or forces may be intent upon helping people, still in partial bondage to their culture and tradition, to break through. If there have already been drastic attempts to free oneself from Saturnian bondage—attempts which have left serious psychological scars—these higher types of psychic factors may become healing agencies. To the 'psychic' experiencing the flow of healing power, they often seem to be 'departed souls' living on 'the other side' and eager to help struggling human beings on 'this side'.

Many interpretations of what is involved in para-psychological occurrences and psychic or spiritual healing are possible, and in spite of the astronauts' landings on the Moon, which they physically experienced as a barren globe of sand and rocks, the real nature of our one and only satellite remains a great mystery—a mystery perhaps hidden in the extraordinary fact that from the Earth the discs of the Sun and the full Moon appear to be of practically the same size. This fact (which is what makes total eclipses possible) is indeed extraordinary, for it means that the small Moon had to be just close enough to the Earth so that it appears to be the same size as the far bigger and more distant Sun.

A polarization is evidently indicated, and at the level of the individual the Sun-Moon polarity points to that of the individualized will and a collective psychic power which is still much of a mystery. Some people may call it 'soul', others (with Carl Jung) the 'anima'. It is, I believe, the *counterpart* of the principle of individuality. We shall see, in Chapter 5, what role it plays when a new process begins which leads from the individual state, the 'I', to a trans-individual condition of being.

In the birth-charts of men and women trying conscious-ly to meet problems and opportunities related to the process of individualization and at least temporary disengagement from collective values, the planet Mercury plays a most important role. It gives mental formulation to the solar will. It seeks to impersonalize and provide a conceptual foundation—a *raison d'etre*— for the often unclear (because emotional) urge the would-be individual experiences to live his or her own life.

This urge is seen in its emotional and personal aspect in the position of and the relationship between Mars and

Venus. In these planets we can see symbolized what the drive toward individualization produces in the personality and consciousness of the 'self-actualizing' human being seeking to assert (Mars) his or her own 'difference', and to revalue (Venus) what his or her family and culture had impressed as being moral or immoral, beautiful or ugly, socially acceptable or unacceptable.

At such a level of interpretation, Saturn, at least potentially, becomes the active power of the Father-within, the 'law' of one's own being. But the center of that individualized, or individualizing, being is not a planet; it is symbolized, I repeat, by the central crossing of horizon and meridian. This I-center finds in Saturn the power to stabilize, steady, and insure the validity of its deep sense of *uniqueness*—its 'identity'. Saturn certifies, if not the new name the individual may have adopted, at least the 'self-image' he or she is building.

Jupiter may refer to the manner in which the social status and group experiences of the individual have contributed to the urge to develop a realization of uniqueness. Jupiter is also the pride engendered by the process of individualization—a pride needed, at least at the beginning of the process, to overcome the fear that individualization may prove too painful or a tragic failure. This pride can nevertheless, later on, become a great obstacle to further growth, because it can cut the individual 'I' off from the power of its roots and insulate it from the descent of spiritual and transformative forces. At this individual level of consciousness, Jupiter can indeed have a more insidiously negative meaning than Saturn, because it tends to fill the Saturnian structure of individual selfhood with an ever-increasing feeling of achievement and a desire for fame and adulation. At the biological level, Jupiter too often leads to excess in eating and overweight. At the individual level, it may produce an over-estimation of one's importance, an unjustifiable Messianic complex, or even a paranoid attitude. As we have seen, it is at the sociocultural level that Jupiter can most beneficially and constructively operate, because it is essentially the 'social' planet.

When a birth-chart is interpreted at the individual level, Uranus, Neptune, and Pluto can play two very different roles. They can be interpreted as extensions of the individual person in his or her relation to society and cultural processes, or as relentless disturbers of the personality and the individual's peace of mind.

Uranus, in the first and positive sense, symbolizes the potential 'genius' of the individual; and by genius I simply mean the capacity a person has to impress vividly upon the collective mind of his culture or community a vision or ideal which has 'come to' him from a source of whose nature he is not clearly (if at all) aware. The 'I-conscious' individual has emerged from his or her natal cultural matrix and is most eager to do his 'own thing'. The individual, even though willing to learn from the past of the culture, is intent upon expressing himself (or herself) in an original and creative manner—upon leaving his mark on society, or at least upon a few individuals to whom he has become close and an 'inspiration'. To do so in a strictly professional sense is to do it at a sociocultural level in terms of what one has learned. This is the application of, in the broad sense of the terms, craftsmanship or professional skill. It refers to 'talent', but not to 'genius'. Talent is a sociocultural factor; genius, the mark of a truly individualized person—unless it manifests in a strictly mediumistic manner, in which case one can speak of 'possession', such as occurred in prophethood or shamanistic performances at the tribal level.

In an individual's birth-chart, Uranus represents the area and the conditions in which the 'genius' of the individual *may* find expression. Nothing in astrological terms, however, can show whether this expression will be significant for anyone beside the individual. The expression may satisfy only the need the individual has to reach beyond the sociocultural level and prove to himself that he is indeed an individual. This need has nevertheless a transformative character, as far as this single person is concerned. If the act or work of genius can transform a whole community or an entire culture, then it is truly linked with a manifestation (however limited and temporary) of the vast movement of human evolution. The individual may believe that what he created has such a meaning, but he does not really experience the source of the creative influx as a transcendent entity or power unless he has already reached beyond the strictly individual level.

This cannot occur as long as the mandala of personality has, as it were, a solid center. The personality is not only strictly defined and limited by its circumference—its outer form; it is also closed to inner influences that would affect its center. The I-center has to 'open up' if transcendent and transindividual power and light is to flow into the mind and eventually the entire personality. Nevertheless, a *pressure* may be experienced which may be called an 'inspiration' or an intuition. It might be symbolized in some cases as an osmotic seeping of the substance of a supermental reality into an individual consciousness sufficiently relaxed to allow this to happen. This gradual 'seeping' should more specifically be interpreted as a Neptunian, rather than Uranian, process. Uranian events generally have a more explosive or lightning-like character. They are, at least at first, particularly experienced at the circumference of being. There, a ruthless conflict may take place between Saturn, seeking to maintain securely and at whatever cost the outer form and inner stability of the being, and Uranus' revolutionary impacts.

From the materialist's point of view, the revolutionary events which produce a breakdown of either a society or an individual person are thought to be 'up-heavals', not unlike volcanic eruptions; and undoubtedly such upheavals can readily occur when experiences which the ego had refused to admit to the field of consciousness have accumulated as 'repressed psychic contents' in dark regions of the personality—the Freudian subconscious or Jung's personal unconscious. Such repressed psychic material and the energy it potentially contains are not unlike toxins accumulating in the body, occasionally flaring up when biological energy is at a low ebb or under attack by an outside force. Yet the fundamental causes of the most significant and ineluctable Uranian crises should rather be sought in a realm that transcends merely personal repressions.

Generally speaking, whenever the possibility for any system of organization (a living entity) to operate at the next higher level has opened up because a new evolutionary cycle had begun, a state of tension develops in that living system. This tension spreads—at first in an unnoticeable manner—throughout the system, and slowly but gradually increases. A whole society and the leaders of its culture experience restlessness and a deep discontent which need only a catalyst to explode. A mere spark of indignation caused by a scandal, a book, or poem that somehow hits a sensitive spot can be such a catalyst, as well as widespread hunger or poverty having reached an apparently unbearable level. The deepest cause of the explosion is the simple fact that a new cycle has started, releasing in a public form new dreams and hopes able to fire the collective imagination of human beings. Thus the famous saying: "Nothing is more powerful than an idea whose time has come."

The Uranian revolutionary is an individual in whom certain personal factors have produced an unusual sensitivity to the change of rhythm caused by the opening of a new planetary cycle. If such an individual is not conscious of this sensitivity, and even less of what planetary and historical cycles are, then Uranus can only operate (symbolically speaking) within his or her closed-centered field of consciousness. The individual considers what he or she does and thinks as being his or her own, even if the feeling is strong in his or her consciousness that somehow the idea or impulse to act has 'come to' him or her. In whatever way it may be believed to have come, the activity is bound to cause some sort of crisis; and the events it spawns may be strongly cathartic.

With Neptune, we are dealing not so much with critical events as with slow, persistent, and perhaps insidious changes. While Uranus may try to batter down the fortified walls of the Saturnian ego, Neptune tends to dissolve them. It has therefore been called the Universal Solvent and its erosionary operation compares to the slow but repeated action of sea waves upon the rocks of the shore. If Uranus refers to the restless discontent with conditions as they *are* and have been for a long time, Neptune evokes the appearance in the consciousness of the visionary image of what *might be* or *should be*. The Neptunian individual tends to be the dreamer of utopias.

His or her function in a culture is important because man cannot actually produce what he has not first imagined, imprecise though the images may have been.

To these Neptunian imaginings Pluto, in its positive aspect, brings concreteness and also a degree of fanaticism. Pluto is the ideologist. For the Plutonian individual, everything has to be decided and acted upon the basis of great impersonal, or rather superpersonal, principles. Pluto brings the universal into the particular, the cosmos into the human person. This can be magnificent or devastating—and at times *both*. If Pluto has often been given a bad reputation in astrological circles, it is because its symbolic action is utterly unsentimental and unconcerned with personal feelings. The sentimentality and constant concern with personal values and issues so evident in our present American culture can be seen as a reaction against the fact that human beings are now confronted with the insistent need of making decisions requiring the understanding of large scale planetary and cosmic principles; and most people are frightened by having to deal with such vast—and to them incomprehensible— issues. In panic they cling to the ropes that bind persons to an elusive play of attraction and repulsion. The ropes constantly break, love turns into hatred, or, what is worse, selfish indifference.

In the charts of most people, Pluto plays no significant individual role, but only refers to the person's involvement in collective and social or political Plutonian crises. When Pluto performs an important individual function, the individual often tries, consciously or instinctively, to gain personal advantage from these collective crises. Even in a catastrophic inflationary period, some individuals manage to make huge fortunes. The man who gains wealth or power through black market operations or by dealing in dangerous drugs—and also the munitions maker, the 'merchant of death'—may have a Plutonian character. Pluto has also been associated with gang leadership because criminal gangs are the products of disintegrating social conditions, which have a Neptunian character. The idealistic and, at the present stage of social and cultural evolution, mostly unrealistic stage of social and cultural evolution, mostly unrealistic concept of egalitarianism is Neptunian. Necessary as it undoubtedly is when Saturnian rigidity and Jupiterian privileges have become static and meaningless, the Neptunian process of leveling down leads to social chaos and the negation of all functional differentiation—a necessity in any organized system of activity. When this occurs, Pluto has to act. It acts positively when it clearly formulates new principles of cosmic order to serve as a foundation for a new society —or, at the individual level, for a new personality and a new body. Pluto acts negatively when the individual uses chaos to gather around his or her ego and totally dominate a blind collectivity of lost souls eager for order and personal contact at any cost.

## Going Beyond the Individual Level

In the preceding discussion of the symbolic characters and meanings of Uranus, Neptune, and Pluto, I have already gone beyond the strictly individual level of human consciousness and life-responses, because I referred these planets to a process of transformation which affects the deepest roots of individual being—the transpersonal process that leads to a fourth level of activity and consciousness, a level beyond the individual. I did this because the value of a strictly individualistic type of consciousness and even of actual experience is today being challenged by worldwide events and possibilities which can hardly be ignored, even by the most individualistic human beings intent on self-fulfillment regardless of what may be working against it. We can, however, observe Uranus, Neptune, and Pluto as they operate in a more restricted sense. They can indeed operate, as it were, at the service of the individual self seeking to actualize as fully as possible its potential of birth as a particular human being in a particular environment. They do so when their activity balances that of Mars, Jupiter, and Saturn.

As I have pointed out in several places,* Uranus can be seen to be the power that constantly opposes the conservative and security-obsessed activity of Saturn by producing minor shocks and crises compelling the mind to overcome its formalism and traditional assumptions, and by inciting the consciousness and feelings to open themselves to new ideals and broader viewponts or more inclusive attitudes. Neptune, on the other hand, counteracts the social ambition and unrestrained expansiveness of Jupiter; it seeks to depersonalize the motives of the individual and to give a more universalistic and humanitarian quality and character to the ideal of individual fulfillment. As to Pluto we can see this often cathartic and relentless planet performing a useful function as the purifier of Martian desires and impulses— a a purification taking the form of a repudiation of all that does not strictly belong to the character and temperament of the individual.

In other words, the three trans-Saturnian planets impel, and sometimes even compel, the self-actualizing individual to overcome the inertia of old biological and social habits—even the inertia implied in self-satisfaction with past achievements which marked only minor steps on the road to the fulfillment of all the possibilities inherent in the individual nature. Yet at the level of individual selfhood, these transformative planets do not fully reveal their essential character, simply because the central 'I' finds it impossible to imagine that it could be 'more-than-I'. The individual may eagerly strive to fulfill his or her personality; but what in the individualized consciousness says 'I' finds it nearly impossible to accept not being the central power to which has to be referred all that the mandala of personality contains. The 'I' can accept Uranus, Neptune, and Pluto only if they act as inspirers, inventors, light-bringers, mind expanders—and all their activities have to be directed toward the superb fulfillment of the experience and feelings of being a unique and creative individual self.

---

*Mainly in my book, *The Sun is Also a Star: The Galactic Dimension of Astrology* (New York, A.S.I.)

One might say that such a feeling of uniqueness is no different from what I have previously described as the ego-feeling, but there is a basic, even if outwardly subtle, difference. *The ego operates at the sociocultural level* and is mainly concerned with preserving the form and security of the boundaries of the human being as a person able to keep successfully alive in a physical and social environment. The *individualized and self-conscious 'I'* cares mostly for its central position and the fact that it should be the ultimate authority in all personal decisions. The ego is moved by fear, and often by guilt, a by-product of fear; the I-center is moved by pride. It will accept any transformation that gives more prestige or power to the personality, but only if that prestige and power serve to magnify the feeling of being-I. The transformative process must not endanger the centrality and the supreme importance of the 'I am' realization. Transformation must be for the purpose of greater fulfillment as an individual. And the individual cannot conceive that such a fulfillment should be regarded as a preliminary step leading to a radical and utterly renewing metamorphosis of all the implications of being.

Yet the possibility of such a metamorphosis is what characterizes the *human* stage in planetary evolution. As I have already stated Man, archetypally considered, represents a stage of transition between 'life' and 'light'— between dark planets and radiant stars. Man is planetary matter on its way to becoming the stellar energy we call light. Man is the 'alchemical vessel' in which matter can be transmuted into spirit.

When Man appears on the stage of planetary evolution —whether on our Earth or on any other dark planet—the phase of biological organization of physical materials (atoms, molecules, cells) has already proven successful. Next comes the stage of collective cultural organization, which has been going on with varying success for millennia. Then, on the foundations built by life and culture, the process of individualization begins to operate. This process has so far been a rather disconcerting and questionable mixture of success and failure. More than the other stages, it has a transitional character because it represents the point at which two opposite currents can meet. The meeting occurs, however, in conditions of extreme instability and with the possibility of unpredictable results.

There are *two* currents. What we interpret today as 'evolution' is only one of them. The complete process of existence is a two-way process. *Spirit descends toward matter as matter rises toward spirit.* The individual is the place of meeting; but it is a difficult meeting. The individualized human self seeks to perpetuate itself, believing itself the summit of evolution, the crown of existence. It craves for fulfillment *as a separate, unique individual.* It clings to what it calls 'my identity'. As long as it can, it remains blind to the power and light that comes 'down' to meet its precarious and inherently tragic eminence. The center of the mandala of personality remains closed to anything but what can be referred to it by the conscious mind.

Eventually, the stubborn and proud refusal to admit the existence of and, to meet what is beyond the individuality and its closed circle of being, must give way to an increasingly open attitude. But this is a difficult, often cathartic, and critical process—a transpersonal process. For whomever is experiencing it, the meaning of almost everything one had neatly characterized and evaluated inelectably changes; new needs take form, new problems have to be solved.

In order to meet them significantly, the astrologer-psychologist has to reinterpret whatever data he or she uses. A transpersonal approach to both astrology and psychology has to be developed. It can only be successfully practiced if based on a genuine and thorough understanding of what is really at stake once the individual opens up to the descent of spiritual, supermental forces. Such an understanding requires an at least partial or tentative realization of the nature of the spiritual Source from which the subliminal light and the transcendent power flow. This light and power may be directly experienced by the fully open individual consciousness, but the Source itself can only be envisioned or evoked through the intermediary of some kind of symbol, image or *mythos.*

For an astrology that has long considered a human

being as a miniature solar system, the state of being beyond the individual is most significantly symbolized by our galaxy, the Milky Way—an immense cosmic organism of radiant stars. One human individual can be imagined to correspond to each of these stars, and an individual's star is symbolically the star exactly at the Zenith at the place and time of birth. In the Christ-mythos, it is the Star of Bethlehem, the Christ-star that represents the divine Identity of Jesus, the totally open individual—the supreme product and apex of human evolution, thus symbolically speaking, the 'Son' of archetypal Man. The transpersonal way—or in the symbolism of esoteric traditions 'the Path' —if successfully trodden, leads to the 'divine Marriage', the union of the Son of Man and the Son of God; and the word God is here but a symbol to evoke the ineffable reality of a transhuman and divine state of being.

# 5

# THE MARRIAGE OF MIND AND SOUL

The basic concept of transpersonal astrology, and also of a kind of psychology using the term transpersonal (in the sense I have used it), is that when a human being has reached a truly individualized and autonomous state of being and consciousness, he or she becomes a 'place' at which two currents of opposite directions will eventually meet: the 'descent' of spirit and the 'ascent' of matter. These two currents answer a fundamental cosmic need which their union will solve. They are synchronous and essentially interdependent. They start operating at the beginning of a world-cycle when a 'divine' creative Act occurs. What is then undifferentiated *proto-matter*—the dust of previous universes, scattered through Space and totally inert—begins to react to the creative Impulse.

This Impulse operates at first in large, simple, whirling movements incessantly repeated. These gradually overcome the inertia of the proto-matter which begins to follow patterns of atomic organization in response to the rhythms of the Creative Impulse. In time the impulse differentiates and a variety of dynamic motions develop, each representing a particular aspect of the vast cosmic idea—the Word or Logos—that had caused the creative Act to occur. Synchronously, material systems progressively evolve toward more complex states of organization within which gradually higher, more inclusive forms of consciousness develop.

When seen from a broad, cosmic, cyclic point of view, the development of material forms of existence and consciousness can be considered symmetrical with the progressive differentiation of the original creative Impulse, but the material entities—though possessing a rudimentary kind of consciousness corresponding to their own level of organization and activity—are completely unaware of the presence of the spiritual forces that are *involving* themselves into essences or archetypal qualities of being, while these material entities are *evolving* toward ever more complex and sensitive modes of existence.

When the process of evolution reaches the human stage, the involuting spiritual archetypes have become sufficiently differentiated for a one-to-one relationship between one of them and a particular human being to be *possible*. This constitutes a basically new situation. The 'downward' current of spirit and the 'upward' current of material organization have become, as it were, close enough eventually to unite. Yet enormous difficulties have still to be met, as the type of consciousness existing in the very first races of human beings is a strictly generic type of consciousness totally controlled by biological forces. Matter has become alive, but in the first humans, 'life' is the absolute ruler. A new power able to serve as a mediator between spirit and life has to manifest. The spiritual current, having broken up into a multitude of differentiated rhythmic units (archetypal qualities of being), and the evolutionary current having then produced human beings totally dominated by a biological type of organization, still operate in opposite directions and with basically different rhythms. They need not only an intermediary to correlate their activities, but a 'place' in which a process of harmonization may be given a definite form, and the purpose of their integration may be made evident to both of them. This intermediary and this place of meeting is what we call *mind*.

Mind simply represents the possibility for spirit and matter to unite within a definite area of experience, and by uniting to fulfill the purpose of the creation of a universe. The essential function of mind is to bring about and stabilize *relationship*. But the work of establishing relationships between forces of opposite polarities is enormously difficult, when these forces are manifesting as an immense variety of forms and tendencies, each displaying a resistance to change. It has to proceed by stages; and real progress can all too often be made only when a disastrous total breakdown—the flying apart of spirit from matter or vice versa—is clearly seen as the only alternative to at least one progressive little step in the process of union.

Mind has to be developed through an associative and integrative process which leads to the formation of a culture fostering the development of collective forms of consciousness. Mind requires a language and the participation of a multitude of human bodies in collective acts; it makes use of man's ability to transfer the results of his experience from generation to generation—the 'time-binding' capacity which according to Count Korzsybsky characterizes the human state.* Mind requires the use of symbols that become, as it were, the 'soul'—the binding factor—of a community. But besides the development of mind, another step is still necessary: the individualization of human beings as singular centers of consciousness and activity. Only a single individual can meet in a state of full, stable consciousness and offer a permanent foundation for an equally differentiated and individualized single manifestation of spirit.

After the final union—at first there may be only brief and temporary meetings—spirit as the positive factor determines the character and function of the being that results from the union of the two currents. This being presumably retains a human (male or female) form, but is now a *transindividual* being. The energies of life still operate in it, though in a profoundly transformed manner, because as long as the organism is made up of chemical earth-materials, it still functions according to the basic rhythms of the biosphere. Yet the power of spirit not only can repolarize and dynamize anew the waning energies of life, but even, if necessary for a specific purpose, substitute for them.

---

*Count Alfred Korzsybski, *The Manhood of Humanity.* (Institute of General Semantics)

The mind of the transindividual being is even more transformed, at least in its deepest aspect, because it no longer needs the symbols which its culture had produced and forcefully impressed upon the child and maturing adult. The transindividual mind can use these symbols, but it is now consciousness free from the psychic bondage to particular symbols and the need to formulate experiences in words, images, or external actions. It is a consciousness that belongs to a level beyond not only the personal ego, but beyond the individual I-center of a closed mandala of personality. I have referred to such a consciousness as *pleroma consciousness*—the Greek gnostic term pleroma referring to a superindividual and spiritual level of being which one could also characterize as 'divine'.*

The mind that uses words and symbols according to the dictates of a particular culture—or today perhaps of a blend of several cultures—is actually responsible for the development and stabilization of the feeling-realization 'I am'. It gives to this feeling-realization a definite and often rigid form. Without this mind, the I-feeling would have no lasting power, somewhat as the President in the White House has power because of the administrative and decision-enforcing bureaucracy and police (or army) that supports him. In a very real sense, the 'I' is a symbol created by the mind on the foundation of a biological feeling or organismic unity and well-being. By contrast, the ego is simply one of the many functions of the physical organism, when the organism operates under the conditions of family, social, religious, and cultural living: the function of insuring security and conditions of existence as stable as possible.

---

*Yet the term *divine* does not necessarily have to have a Judeao-Christian religious meaning, that is, to be applied only to the one and only God, Creator of the universe. In ancient religions, many gods are mentioned, who are different aspects of a supreme cosmic being. In his great book, *The Life Divine*, Sri Aurobindo evokes the possibility that humanity may one day be composed of beings who could truly be considered divine.

Yet, in another sense, the experience of 'I am'—'I am a totally integrated being functioning as an autonomous, independent and responsible being'—means that the current of material evolution has reached its apex. Within the once scattered, inert, and indifferent units of matter, the universal power of integration, which I call ONE or SELF, is now a dominant Presence. But it is a power limited by *the physicality* of what it has integrated. It is power at work in dark substance and always confronted with the violence of biological forces and the conflicts of the sociocultural world. It works through a mind bound by the very symbols it uses—symbols which refer to experiences in the biosphere of a dark planet. This mind as yet does not realize that in the cosmic scheme it is meant to be the consecrated place—a sacred enclosure, a temple—in which a basically different and far more crucial type of integration, that of spirit and matter, has to occur.

This temple, however, has to be built using the symbolic materials—words and ideas—of a culture that arose out of collective experiences. The mind had to be collective before it could be truly individual. It had to be rationalistic and logical in order to attain an objective consistency before it could become the intuition and vision of a Seer. Therefore, when the individual stage of human existence is reached, great questions—which most individuals try not to ask—arise: What is this mind *for?* What purpose are the psychic forms it has built to serve?

What makes the situation so difficult and confusing is that the mind itself has to formulate the answers to its own reluctantly-asked questions, for *nothing else could.* Yet, if left alone, the mind would give either a collective, biological, and cultural answer or, by glorifying the I-feeling as the absolute culmination of the universal process of existence, it would close the door of the field of consciousness to the downflow of spiritual forces. A factor existing within the human psyche beside the mind has somehow to act directly upon the mind, or to serve as a hidden gate through which 'inspirations' of a spiritual nature may enter and gradually transform the mind.

I have referred to this factor (Chapter 4, p. 88) as a force that can operate as a counterpart to the principle of individualization. From the point of view of the individualizing person and his or her conscious and objective mind, this force acts in a quite mysterious and dark area of the psyche which psychologists like to call 'the Unconscious'. This area is outside of the field of consciousness of such a person because this field is entirely occupied with either the process of dealing with the biosocial and cultural environment, or that of furthering individualization through the use of intellectual operations. Nevertheless, this area outside of the field of consciousness is an integral part of the whole person and is most likely linked in some way with a particular area in the body whose exact location seems to be a controversial subject.

This counter-individual factor might be called the 'soul', but this word is confusing since it has been used in so many ways. What Jung called the 'anima' can be related to it, but anima has a more restricted meaning and belongs to a different approach to psychology from the one I am developing here. As I see it, the function of the soul is to serve as a base of operation for the higher type of integration—the integration of spirit and matter—during the periods in which the mind is entirely occupied with the processes of cultural, personal, and individual integration.

The soul has a collective, psychic aspect which operates in the religious sphere as true faith and devotion. It 'ensouls' religious practices and observances. It is very active in the lives of the great religious mystics, the great dreamers of an absolutely transcendent state of unity, who, by intensifying their feeling-nature, attempt to by-pass the stage of individual selfhood and to raise their consciousness directly from the cultural to the transcendent (or 'divine') level, and eventually to reach a 'unitive state' of identification with what their religions call God in many languages. This mystic way and the bhakti path which has dominated the culture of India (and to a much lesser extent the European Middle Ages), seem to me to represent only one phase of the total process of raising human consciousness to a state beyond individuality. It should have to be balanced at one time or another—in preceding or subsequent lives—by the development of the individualizing mind.

As long as the autocratic power of the I-center totally dominates and controls the closed mandala of personality, the mind is most often blinded by that power. The mind can only begin to become aware of the deepest and ultimate purpose it is meant to serve when the 'I am' power of integration tends to break down, finding it too difficult to cope with crucial problems of life as an individual in constant conflict with other individuals within an increasingly chaotic society. When, at the same time, another kind of power operating *through* the soul exerts constant pressure upon the mind and perhaps is able to penetrate its rigid structure with flashes of inspiration and intuition, the mind gradually—or in some cases suddenly—realizes its bondage to the 'I am' center, and the nature of its higher function. It begins to work at building the inner temple under the impulsion of the power it dimly senses operating through the soul. This power is, symbolically speaking, that of the zenith-star—a light-radiating entity belonging to a more-than-individual level of existence—the level at which the spiritual reality of Humanity-as-a-whole has its being.

In astrological symbolism, this is the level of existence represented by our galaxy, the Milky Way. The star whose light and power first radiates through the soul and eventually illumines the mind represents the trans-individual state of existence of the human being. The *potentiality* of that state has been inherent in every human being for perhaps millions of years; but it is still, for most human beings living today, *only a distant potentiality*. The greatest part of mankind is still hesitantly, and most often blindly, working to actualize this possibility. The process of actualization which began at the biological level proceeded through the sociocultural level to the stage of autonomous individual selfhood. This state does *not* constitute the final 'human condition'. The I-consciousness can and in time will lead the whole of humanity to a '*We*' -consciousness—pleroma consciousness.

This 'We' is totally different from the biological 'we' of the family group or the social 'we' of an aristocratic class responsible for the maintenance and glorification of a particular culture. In the pleroma state, the consciousness of all participants *interpenetrate*. There are no more individual barriers, yet the resulting unanimity should not negate any sense of individuality. The pleroma is a totally integrated orchestra of beings who nevertheless can act as individuals in the fulfillment of the role that each is to play in the performance of Man.

At this time in human history, the relation between mind and soul is of particular importance; much depends upon how it is interpreted. Because our Western society has so greatly stressed the development of the objective, analytical mind, a strong reaction to thinking has lately developed, inspired or at least strengthened by the spread of Oriental philosophy and the fascination exerted by various types of 'spiritual Teachers' from Asia. Mental activity has been downgraded, and the word soul is used to glorify a non-mental type of either emotional feeling or of a 'spiritual' way of life. If we return to what I have stated in the first chapter of this book, we could readily interpret this resurgence of all that can be covered by the word soul as an indication that the Yin approach to life has begun to rise in strength after the Yang approach had reached its apex. Characteristic expressions of the Yang principle are the Euro-American collective mind, with its intense eagerness to control the material environment through intellectual knowledge, and what Oswald Spengler called the Faustian spirit, a restless spirit intent on the conquest of whatever is beyond the familiar and the known. Thus we can see in the soul a principle of compensation for the mind's tendency to dominate the field of activity and the consciousness of modern human beings. Such an interpretation, however, does not give a complete picture of the situation.

A mind is simply a form of consciousness. More precisely, it is a more or less clearly and sharply defined 'area' (an awkward term to be understood symbolically rather than geometrically) within the total field of activity we call a human being. When this field is not only well-organized at the biological level as a body, but also at the sociocultural level as a person embodying in a particular way a collective psyche, a new trend begins to develop. The process of individualization starts. This process *uses* the mind to achieve its purpose, for mental activity is necessary to build a complex structure of consciousness from which the new principle of individual selfhood, the 'I', can operate. In principle, the 'I' operates simply as a centralizing and integrative factor; but as the necessity of overcoming the inertia of what biology and culture have built is felt, the 'I' also apparently finds it necessary to act forcefully or cleverly to rule, and to enforce the laws and regulations the mind formulated. The 'I' becomes a more or less absolute king or monarch.

Such a domination requires the individualization of consciousness. Consciousness, which was collective and psychic at the sociocultural level, becomes individualized through an enhanced operation of the objective, analytical mind. This individualization of a consciousness and psychism which had been almost entirely collective during long periods of human evolution quite obviously produces resistance. This resistance to the individualization of consciousness and the collective psyche gives form to a 'soul'. Within this soul *two* distinct forces are at work, though most people do not differentiate them. One of these forces is the power of tradition—the power of what still operates as collective psychism in the community in which the individual-in-the-making was born. The other force emanates from a *higher collectivity*—the 'greater whole' in which all human beings 'live, move, and have their being,' *though for a long time they are not aware of this fact*. This higher collectivity is Humanity-as-a-whole as an all-inclusive planetary reality of which the world of physical matter is *only of several aspects*.

This higher collectivity exists in a state of consciousness that transcends *both* the collective consciousness of a culture-whole and that of human beings having reached the status of truly autonomous individuals; yet, both the cultural and the individual stages are necessary to its actualization. I have already referred to this transcendent state of consciousness as pleroma consciousness. The power that operates within the soul is the energy and light of this pleroma consciousness. In other words, the light and power of the greater whole Humanity (in the all-inclusive sense of the term) acts within the soul of every individualized person. It has to act in order to counteract the individualizing trend; for if Humanity-as-a-whole did not act, the drive toward the fulfillment of individual selfhood would inevitably develop an irresistible momentum and crystallize into a rigid and tyrannical power—the unchecked power of the individual self, the 'I am'.

To say that this power is that of the ego is, I repeat, to fail to understand the difference between the sociocultural and the individual levels of activity. Such a failure often leads to much psychological confusion. It clouds up the nature of the soul.

The soul—I repeat—has a collectivistic, traditional aspect; and all institutionalized religions are based on and thrive from it. But it also serves as a *base of operation* for the greater whole Humanity in its attempt to keep the force of individualization (the Yang power) from producing an unyielding, utterly proud 'I' backed, and also to a large extent controlled, by the patterns and devices of a bureaucracy of the mind. Thus Yang and Yin do not refer primarily to mind and soul. They rather symbolize the power that produces the emergence of individuals out of collective culture-wholes, and the power of the greater whole that seeks to bring all these individuals to the realization that they are potentially, and therefore have to become, co-participants in its vast field of activity and consciousness far transcending the individual state of existence.

Let me stress again that both powers are equally necessary in order for the process of transition from level to level to take place. A human being must pass through the stage of conscious individualization before he or she consciously and responsibly participate in the activity of Humanity-as-a-whole. Human consciousness has to become focused through a clear and individually centered and structured mind; but this focusing and centering and individualization of consciousness has also to be balanced by a drive for transformation and transmutation, or it could take a monstrous form which would negate the possibility of the development of consciousness at a higher, more inclusive level. Thus the individual should tone down his or her sense of achievement and the pride it engenders, so that he or she is able to listen to the 'voice' of the soul, and by relaxing what Carl Jung graphically called the 'cramp in the conscious' to open himself or herself to the downflow of light and transcendent energy which passes through the soul. I repeat, the soul does not generate this transformative current of spiritual power. The power comes from the greater whole—the planetary Being, Humanity-as-a-whole.

This planetary Being exists at a level that transcends the individual state, and therefore should be thought of as a pleroma of unanimous and spiritually integrated centers rather than as a supreme Person to whom the religious consciousness of human individuals gives the name God. Yet *in relation to a human individual*, this divine pleroma actually assumes what to the individual is felt to be a 'personal' character. When 'God' speaks to a man or woman, He becomes personalized in terms of the particular *need* of the human being, or of the individual character of the cultural or spiritual work he or she may be charged to perform according to his or her special talent.

This fact, which has seemed so mysterious and awesome to many European thinkers and mystics, can be made more understandable—because it is de-glamorized—if we see it in the light of astrological symbolism. When an individualized human being is represented by the solar system as a whole, the transindividual, divine pleroma becomes symbolized by the galaxy, the Milky Way, in which the solar system is but a perhaps relatively insignificant atom or cell. Our Sun is a star. Thus every individualized man or woman is also *potentially* a divine being, a small unit within the divine pleroma, Humanity-as-a-whole—and symbolically a star in the galaxy.

We have seen that the principle of individual selfhood, the 'I', is the center of the mandala of personality—the birth-chart. As this center 'looks up' to the sky, it should be able to discover the galactic star it *potentially* is. The star is therefore symbolically the one exactly at the zenith. The transpersonal way is the pathway that leads from the center of the chart to this star at the zenith. On this pathway, the divine power and light of this 'star' come down to meet the individual as the individual ascends toward it. A two-way, broadly symmetrical process is at work. In religious terms, God comes toward Man as human beings who have become conscious individuals aspire and reach toward God, in ardent prayer and all-consuming love.

Seen from a purely psychological point of view, this process takes the form of a coming together and interpenetration of soul and mind. The mind dominates the entire field of consciousness whose center is the individualized self, 'I'. Thus, as I have already stated, to this conscious I-center the soul at first inevitably appears to be *outside* of the field of consciousness. Whether this soul is said to be 'in the depth' of the psyche or the highest part of it, it is still outside of the field whose contents can be referred to the I-center in conscious and more or less rationally formulatable terms—or if not entirely outside, then in an area that joins the field of consciousness to the unconscious.

What Carl Jung called the *anima* is defined as a function of mediation between the conscious and the unconscious —an intermediary, a link. In a limited sense, it corresponds to what I have called the soul here; but where Jung and I radically differ is in our conception of what operates through the soul—what is beyond it. He speaks of the Collective Unconscious and the realm of Archetypes; Goethe before him mentioned in a somewhat similar sense the realm of 'the Mothers'. On the other hand, according to the cosmic concept of 'holarchy' I present, what is beyond the soul and uses it to serve as a base of operation at the level of individualized human personalities, is Humanity as a spiritual Being encompassing all individuals—a Pleroma of consciousness and activity existing at a transindividual level. All individualized persons can reach this level, but only if their minds not only become aware of the reality of the soul, but accept to include this reality in the field of consciousness and persuade the I-center to open itself and welcome the unfamiliar and often disturbing experiences resulting from the admission of the soul into the field of consciousness. When this occurs, a psychologically transforming process which Jung calls "the assimilation of the contents of the Unconscious" and "the process of individuation" begins to operate.

It may operate relatively smoothly, but most of the time it requires a series of crises. In some instances, the mind may open itself readily to let the newcomer enter the field of consciousness, but feeling the resistance of the individual center to the implications of the soul's messages, the mind often subtly intellectualizes or personalizes the transcendent soul-revelations of a higher, 'divine' state of existence so as to make them acceptable to the 'I'. The I-center might be willing to reverently bow before a higher, more powerful kind of individual person, but only if by doing so it still remains 'I', king in its own realm. A king may bow to a still greater emperor, if his station as a king remains officially recognized. Likewise, a human being may devote himself or herself to a great guru, provided he or she is not asked irrevocably to give up his or her essential status as an individual, especially in relation to the other chelas of the guru.

When the mind and the soul fully interpenetrate, the light and power of the greater whole, the pleroma of Humanity, can fully illumine the field of consciousness. The I-center accepts to surrender its central station—its 'throne'. However beautiful and fulfilled the individual self was, it remained a solid and substantial reality with a physical base, the body. The mandala of personality with an enthroned 'I' as its center is a closed-center mandala. It becomes an open-center mandala when the throne of the 'I' dissolves, as it were, under the Neptunian light of the spiritual Pleroma of Man. Through that central void, the light of the 'star'—which our consciousness interprets as our transindividual self—can be seen. Its rays transfigure the mind now united with the soul, and the power of the vast galactic communion of stars reaches down into the biological roots of the human being to gradually transsubstantiate the matter of the cells that life had bound and the mind had often perverted or filled with toxins produced by social ambition or individual vices.

When this process of transsubstantiation is completed, or at least nears completion, a *transindividual being* emerges from the metamorphosis. Such a being operates at a 'transphysical' level. Biological forces no longer operate, or at least not in the way we today think of and observe their operations. The type of 'matter' our senses perceive and our intellect categorizes as 'physical' is transmuted into a subtler kind, to which the imprecise name 'etheric' has often been given. This subtler matter may also refer to what the traditions of India called *akhasa*—a word which has recently become popularized in our Western world, but which seems to be used improperly in many instances.

The existence of transindividual beings can be experienced once an unrestricted openness of the I-consciousness has been achieved, and the karma of the physical and emotional-mental personality makes such an experience possible and safe. It would be neither safe nor possible in a concrete manner if the individual had not first passed through a process of biological and 'magnetic' purification, and if the mind were not fully open to and welcoming the experience without fear. There are, however, various levels of realization—various kinds of experiences that provide an increasingly solid and indisputable foundation for what, at the level of a strictly individual and I-centered consciousness, is at first only an 'intuition'.

When I refer to a trans*personal* individual, I am not speaking of a trans*individual* being, but only of an individual person who has definitely taken steps on the path of radical and total transformation. The *transpersonal way* refers to this path which symbolizes a long and arduous process that can take a great variety of forms, yet which has a definite, nearly universal structure—just as the embryonic development of a future human being, within the mother's womb, takes place according to a series of clearly marked phases. This process of rebirth is difficult and often requires intense phases of catharsis because of the inertia of the biological past and the socio-cultural and individual karma that must be overcome.

All individuals whose minds have opened themselves to the messages or visions that the soul reveals in symbolic forms, and who have accepted the challenge of total transformation, have to undergo such a process of rebirth. In the life of any truly individualized person, a moment always comes when the implications of a basic choice are more or less clearly presented to the I-center. The 'I' has to choose between self-fulfillment as an end in itself, or open-ended transformation. The choice is between straining after greater perfection of form through which the self would be glorified and perhaps immortalized among men, and entering an unfamiliar 'mountainous' path whose end seems always to recede beyond the horizon, and whose challenges are so complex or elusive that the mind is never able precisely to formulate them and deal directly with the problems they pose.

On that path of radical transformation, faith is needed—a faith requiring humility, as well as the courage which can only be born of an inner realization of the irrevocable character of a decision whose source is more than merely mental, because it is in fact the progeny of the psychic 'marriage' of the soul and the mind. The union of mind and soul is a marriage in the true and spiritual sense of a union consecrated by God, for it occurs in the presence, intuitively felt if not clearly perceived, of the star, symbol of the divine state that is latent in every human being. Yet the I-centered consciousness may still be so reluctant to give up its prerogatives that it may refuse to accept the new life-situation for what it is. It is therefore the mind's task to interpret this situation in such a way that the I-consciousness, seeing itself but a phase of a vast cosmic process, will serenely accept being absorbed, yet not dissolved, into a consciousness that emcompasses the entire process and all its temporary phases and achievements—biological, cultural, and individual—yet does not repudiate or negate any of them.

This new task of the mind in union with the soul can be performed in several ways. I think of a transpersonal astrology simply as a significant way for modern individuals to gain a more objective, non-glamorous, and non-devotional understanding of the process of total transformation. In this kind of astrology, every astrological factor has to be referred, not to the individual 'I' enthroned at the closed center of the mandala of personality, but to the process of transformation. Transpersonal astrology is therefore an essentially dynamic kind of astrology.

The birth-chart still remains a fundamental factor for it reveals what the process of transformation starts from and what conditions this process—thus the individual's karma and innate capacities. It also suggests by implication the order in which basic changes and crises are likely to occur and how they are interrelated. However, in terms of the relationship of the astrologer and the client, a greater importance is usually given to 'progressions' and 'transits', that is, *to the process of change itself.* The purpose of astrological interpretation at the transpersonal level is not to give precise information concerning events *in themselves,* or to solve problems of interpersonal relationships *in themselves,* but to reveal how *everything* in daily living can be consciously and understandingly used as a step forward in the transpersonal process.

# 6

## THE PRACTICE OF ASTROLOGY AT THE TRANSPERSONAL LEVEL

In order clearly to understand and practice what a few years ago I began to call 'transpersonal astrology', an astrologer should fully realize what it is *not*. It is not classical European astrology, based on the approach formulated in Alexandria by Ptolemy and later by Roman and Medieval writers. It is not popular fortune-telling. It is not what is now known as esoteric astrology, and it does not deal with what is considered to be a 'soul chart', nor is it Uranian astrology or cosmobiology. Though it is based on the holistic and psychological foundations characterizing the 'humanistic' or 'person-centered' type of astrology I first formulated in the *The Astrology of Personality*, a strictly transpersonal approach to astrology has a different orientation and gives to the astrologer-client relationship a rather unprecedented character. It interprets astrological data in terms of a new set of values.

Transpersonal astrology addresses itself specifically to human beings whose problems and expectations derive from the fact that they are (or consider themselves to be) not only autonomous, self-motivated 'individuals', but individuals who realize that mere satisfaction—the growth and fulfillment of their individuality at a strictly personal and social or cultural level—is not an end in itself. They see in such personal fulfillment and happiness, at best, *a phase* in a transformative process that should lead to a higher and more inclusive level of consciousness and activity, a 'spiritual' state.

Such individuals constitute only a small minority in relation to the masses of mankind, but because our society is now passing through a state of crisis with a potential of either global disaster or radical transformation, the number of individuals who are aspiring to a really new and at least relatively transcendent state of being is steadily increasing. These individuals are experiencing a profound dissatisfaction with present-day conditions not only of living, but of thinking and feeling. They do not want merely to grow bigger and better as personalities, but to become transformed into a new type of human, or an even more-than-human being. They therefore do not find deeply satisfying or especially inspiring and transformative answers in either the now-popular forms of psychology and quasi-psychotherapy represented by humanistic psychologists and the various forms taken by the human potential movement, or in the broadly psychological type of astrology which merely describes their character and how they should handle their conflicts or opportunities for growth at a purely personal level—a kind of growth that would mainly make them feel happier, more confident, and better able to function at home and in various social situations.

As I have stated at the close of the last chapter, an individual today more than ever before may be faced by the need to choose between *fulfillment* as a social person within the collective framework of his or her culture and radical *transformation*. What is usually called 'growth' leads only to a more or less individualized form of fulfillment that does not deeply challenge the collective assumptions of the culture and the way of life of society, or at least of one's peer-group or social class. This kind of growth may modify the character and personality of a human being; it may have extremely valuable results at the psychological level, or even extend the field of consciousness through the blending of several cultures and their approaches to self-development. *But as long as the position of the 'I-center' in the personality remains secure, unchallenged, growth is personal not transpersonal.*

An individual solely, or even primarily, intent upon a personal kind of happiness and fulfillment—what he or she may wish to call 'the integration of personality'—should seek advice and guidance from a person-centered type of astrological interpretation. Such an interpretation is basic, and even an astrologer employing a definitely transpersonal approach has always to keep it in the background.

Both the process of personal growth and the process of transpersonal transformation *start* from the same place: where the client 'is' (or stands). They both have to begin with what he or she congenitally, socially, and individually is, and especially from what his or her mind is able to understand. But from the transpersonal point of view, whatever state of life the individual has reached, and whatever he or she possesses (psychologically speaking), are there *to be used* in the best manner possible to fuel the fire of transformation. On the other hand, in a person-centered type of astrology, all this personal material is considered as a field of more or less undeveloped substance to be refined and interrelated, usually according to the prevailing sociocultural model or plan, in the building of a smoothly operating, loveable, and successful personality.

In both cases, the natal chart provides the fundamental data that have to be considered, but after these data are understood, the focus of attention of the two types of astrologers changes. The person-centered, *humanistic astrologer* thinks of how best to help the harmonious development of the birth-potential along sociocultural lines; the *transpersonal astrologer* tries to evoke (for the individual eager for self-transcendence), the possibility of using every opportunity, every tension, every crisis as means to gradually overcome the inertia of his or her past, of social and mental habits and prejudices and, above all, the resistance of the 'I' to changes that would undermine its centralizing and controlling authority.

While in a person-centered type of interpretation, the process of change is given the basic meaning of the actualization of the innate potentialities defined by the birth-chart, and every progression is seen as an opportunity for growth—easy or difficult as it may be—a transpersonal interpretation considers every step on the road as a particular way of preparing for a radically transformative change. At the individual level of consciousness and activity, self-actualization refers to the fulfillment of what a 'seed' sown *in the past* contains in potentiality. But, from a transpersonal point of view, what takes place during the progress of growth of an infant into adult has *in youth* the purpose of allowing the past (karma, whether 'good' or 'bad') to exhaust its as yet unspent energy, so that *after maturity and midlife*, the individualized consciousness and will may freely and safely repolarize themselves and use every opportunity for self-transformation and a *future* seed-mutation.

The ordinary person thinks he or she looks to the future while striving to actualize and fulfill his or her personality in terms of the goals publicized by society and culture; but what is actualized is a *prolongation*, and in most instances only a superficially modified *repetition*, of the genetic and sociocultural *past*. We have to choose between allegiance to a past we seek to fulfill in our own personal way, and consecration to what for us, as mature human beings, is a possible future state—the transindividual state. Once such a choice is made, every astrological aspect is interpreted as an opportunity for transformation on the way to the 'star'.

Such a transpersonal interpretation of astrological data is in most cases significant and called for only after an individual has reached at least relative maturity. Yet we are today increasingly confronted by children and teenagers (some quite rebellious) who are sensitive to the possibility of radical transformation—even if it is only a naively formulated dream. The old ancestral seed has lost much of its power; the old karma may soon exhaust itself, and this leads to a deep, poignant feeling of emptiness whose cause and meaning are not understood. Then a transpersonal approach can be of great value, if it is adequately and sensitively presented.

The momentum, memory, and attractive power of the ancestral past and the old karmic patterns usually linger on for a long, long time, even when the vision of future possibilities has startled the consciousness, only perhaps to be discounted or laughed at by the mind. Then too can a transpersonal astrological and psychological interpretation be an important factor, for it can help the client gradually to reinterpret all the events of his or her past. By giving a new and transformative meaning to past events— especially past traumas, frustrations, and psychic injuries —the past is actually changed. It is *transpersonalized*. Every tragic occurrence may be consciously understood as a necessary step in the process that may eventually lead to the transindividual state.

The astrologer has first to be *able* to use such a transpersonal approach, but it should be evident that he or she has also to answer to his or her satisfaction a crucial and determining question: is the client *ready*—has he or she the will and, even more than merely the desire, indeed the ability to deal with his or her problems in a transpersonal manner?

## The Client's Readiness and the Astrologer's Responsibility

An astrologer seeking to interpret a birth-chart as a symbol (or hieroglyph) of the possibility of an individual entering upon the path of radical transformation should evidently be thoroughly grounded in the *language* of astrology, whose words are planets, signs, and houses, and whose syntax is provided by the interplanetary aspects—and (in a sense) whose punctuation is provided by the house cusps. The ordinary astrologer is like a prose-writer giving more or less detailed *information*. The transpersonal astrologer is like a poet evoking the *meaning* of the whole chart as a symbol of the whole person and his or her potential of transformative unfoldment.

It is obvious that no one can really teach how to write poetry or define the *qualifications* for being a poet. All that can be taught in school are *the rules used in poetry of a particular culture*—rules that limit the field of expression, but can also deepen this expression by condensing it (as in the Sonnet or the *Haiku* poetry of Japan).

Condensation implies the rejection of all non-essentials. Likewise, I tend to use only the simplest, most essential 'words' in the language of astrology. I pay very little attention to 'new discoveries' which do not fill an evident place in the basic structure of the solar system—for example, the few asteroids now often used simply because some astronomer took the trouble to calculate their orbits. Similarly, in the Occult astrology to which H. P. Blavatsky refers in *The Secret Doctrine* only "sacred planets" are said to be considered, though over a hundred other planets are in existence at one level of physicality or another.

A poet, however, does not usually feel responsible for the feelings his or her poetry may evoke in readers. Yet an author's responsibility can be great. We know historically that the publication of Goethe's *Werther* led to a number of suicides. The astrologer using a transpersonal approach (and no one has any right to call himself or herself "*a* transpersonal astrologer") thus incurs a twofold responsibility. On the one hand, he or she deals directly, face-to-face, with a client. Thus there is a person-to-person relationship and responsibility, as in the case of a consultation with a trained psychologist. Therefore, much depends upon what the person of the astrologer emanates to the client. There are a few 'born astrologers,' but this does *not* mean being 'psychic'. It means instead facility in translating the abstract 'words' of the astrological language into inspiring, evocative, and cohesive meaning, also interpersonal sensitivity or empathy—and openness to 'inner guidance.'

This last-mentioned quality exemplifies the second aspect of responsibility assumed by the astrologer adopting a transpersonal approach, for as one who advocates treading the path of radical transformation he or she speaks for or represents to the client the promptings of the client's higher being and potentialities for transformation. This responsibility is not merely a 'horizontal' one confined to the person-to-person astrologer-client relationship. It is also a 'vertical' or transpersonal one in which the astrologer accepts being the 'agent' or 'mouthpiece' of higher powers urging the client to transform himself or herself, to open the closed center of the mandala of his or her personality to an influx of transcendent power and light. In this sense, the astrologer endeavoring to show the way along the path of radical transformation is indeed a poet, in the broadest sense of the original Greek term: one who acts as a "mover and shaker" of souls.

Let me repeat what I have often stated. Astrology is *not* a science. Transpersonal astrology is not even actually an 'art.' It is a means of communication. The good astrologer is able to communicate meanings. These are grounded in what the astrologer sees in a chart and its progressions and transits with his or her analytical mind (his or her knowledge of the language of communication). Such grounding *never* should take less than a few years of concentrated study not only of the elements of the language of astrology per se, but even more, of well-known people's birth-charts, progressions, and transits in connection with their detailed year-by-year biographies— the only way of intelligently studying the intricacies of actually applying and using astrology.

Assuming that the astrologer has understood, assented to and prepared himself or herself to assume the responsibility of all that is implied in the practice of a transpersonal approach, the actual use of such an approach for a particular client can prove valid, significant, and above all, safe and constructive only if the client already understands to some extent what a basic process of transformation implies, and more or less clearly feels, in the depth of his or her consciousness, the need to deal with long insoluble problems in a new and radical manner. Most of the time, such a feeling comes only after a person has experienced difficult crises and has perhaps been shocked into the realization that a basic change at any cost is imperative—and indeed the only alternative to complete breakdown. Various palliatives or partial solutions have probably been unsuccessfully tried along traditional lines—religious, moral, or psychological. But in our present society, which has lost most of its reliance upon ancient principles of interpersonal relationship and any sense of the 'sacred', traditional solutions are often no

longer convincing and therefore no longer valid or effective. The individual is then left to his or her own devices,
and often seeks help along unconventional lines—perhaps
rushing from one weekend seminar to another or from
one ashram to the next. These excursions may sooner or
later lead to an astrologer. But what does or should the
client expect of an astrological 'reading'?

If a person comes to an astrologer solely out of intellectual curiosity and simply to find out how much the
astrologer will be able to tell concerning past or future
events and character-traits, he or she should certainly *not*
come to an astrologer using a transpersonal approach,
and the astrologer he or she sees should not try to use one.
It would also be far better if the client did not expect the
astrologer to be a substitute father- or mother-figure on
whom the whole responsibility for making decisions
would be placed in a spirit of psychological dependence—
a situation occurring frequently today.

Transpersonal astrology should not be approached with
the expectation that it may *solve* any or all personal
problems. It can only help an individual, confused by a
situation filled with unknown and knowable factors,
*transcend* these problems by clearly, objectively, and
unemotionally understanding where they fit into the
larger, transformative pattern of a step-by-step unfoldment of innate, but mostly latent potentiality. A
psychologist of the human potential movement might
arouse in a long-restrained and static personality the
impulse to develop unused capacities and what is so often
mistakenly called 'creativity' or 'spontaneity.' But this
arousal would, in most instances, have only an emotional
or personal foundation. It would usually operate, at best,
only at the individual level of consciousness and activity.
Nevertheless, this is obviously the highest level at which
the immense majority of human beings today can operate.
The individual who in his or her distress has tried some of
these now-popularized methods may eventually reach an
astrologer known to use a transpersonal approach.

A transpersonal interpretation of astrological data is
not meant to provide the client with set and precise
solutions or recipes for 'spiritual living.' Its basic function

is to *evoke possibilities* emerging out of a new and more inclusive way of understanding not merely a particular situation or conflict, but the *need* or opportunity for transformation the situation suggests or underscores. For such an understanding to be effective, the client's present situation or conflict has to be shown to him or her as a particular phase of a process of transformation whose entire span must also be abstractly surveyed, understood, and subjectively assented to by the I-center of the client's personality.

This may mean that as a preliminary step to a transpersonal interpretation, or to the astrologer's assessing its appropriateness, the astrologer and client together might review the major events, circumstances, and inner turning points in the client's life thus far. This can be significantly enlightening for both the client and the astrologer, especially if such a review takes place against the background of the astrological progressions and major transits of the client's life—for as I have said at the close of the last chapter, transpersonal astrology tends to give a greater importance to the process of change and unfoldment of latent potentialities itself, i.e., to what is represented by astrological progressions and transits, than to what may be symbolized in the birth-chart alone.

For the client, such a review may help to reveal the unquestionable inevitability of entering upon the path of radical transformation, for he or she may come to see how the whole of his or her life has been leading to such a decision. For the astrologer, such a review may enable him or her to at least tentatively answer a crucial question: is the individual whose chart is being studied *ready*, sufficiently *eager*, and at least moderately *able* to safely begin or to pursue farther the process of transformation? Asking and at least tentatively answering this question is indeed crucial, for both the client and the astrologer, for the path of radical transformation, once entered upon, cannot be safely trodden backward, unless it be for the temporary purpose of a 'strategic retreat' or for testing to learn if one has missed the right turn in a deeply confusing situation.

From such a review the astrologer may indeed be able

to determine that the client understands, accepts, and is ready to pursue an interpretation of his or her chart giving a transformative meaning to all the elements of the personality and life-pattern. On the other hand, what may be revealed is an individual still uncertain and confused, one who still needs to pursue goals of social or personal fulfillment. Nevertheless, underlying the client's confusion, apathy, or self-centeredness, the astrologer may perceive an inner strength and soul-directed intuition, which the astrologer can hope to arouse in the client by presenting him or her with a new possibility of existence, a new vision.

Nevertheless, in attempting to assess the client's readiness for a transpersonal interpretation of his or her birth-chart and other astrological data, the astrologer finds himself or herself in a similar position to the one of trying to assess the level at which the client is already operating. He or she must therefore take into consideration all I have said and pointed toward when discussing that problem in Chapter 3, and as well all of the issues I have raised since the opening pages of this chapter.

The fact is that it is extremely difficult for an astrologer to 'know' how his or her client will actually react to any kind of interpretation of the astrological factors involved in any situation being discussed. No one can even be absolutely certain at the level of the mind what his or her own responses will be when being made aware of what at first may seem to be an unfamiliar or, astrologically speaking, a dire prospect just ahead, or the need for a crucial decision requiring severance from some familiar situation. A higher-than-mental kind of 'knowing' should operate in the astrologer; a sense of inevitability should be experienced by the client, making what we love to call 'free choice' actually irrelevant. But such a feeling-experience of inevitability or 'no choice' may not come easily to most people relying strongly upon mental processes in which pro-and-con argumentation predominates; or, if such a feeling arises in the consciousness, it may result from the mind having been so thoroughly indoctrinated in a particular approach to life and problem-solving that there can be no doubt about what is the 'right' judgment or course of action one may take.

In terms of the everyday practice of astrology, all this may simply mean that the transpersonal astrologer—more than the ordinary astrologer who merely describes a client's character and apparent opportunities, strengths and weaknesses—has to rely upon his or her deepest intuition of *what seems possible* for the client. Two or more ways of interpreting past experiences in the client's life, or several alternative courses of action and their expectable consequences in relation to present situations may have to be presented by the astrologer as a way of testing from the immediate reaction or facial expression of the client the character or range of what is possible for him or her.

However, when an astrologer (or psychologist) has taken a definite public stand on the most basic questions involved in the function and practice of astrology (or psychology), it is quite likely that mainly persons who, consciously or unconsciously, *need* what that practitioner has to offer will be attracted to him or her to ask for a consultation. In any case, the astrologer should make his or her position clear at the start, stating to prospective clients what his or her basic approach to astrology and life in general is. Some written statement by the astrologer, which the client is asked to accept, may prove very useful, especially if the legal status of astrology in the place where the consultation is held is doubtful, which is the usual case.

Nevertheless, such a written statement or even a tacit or explicit agreement between the astrologer and the client should not be taken by either party to it as an absolution of responsibility. Anytime a counselor attempts to guide a client—even if he or she simply tries to present the client's problem or situation in a clearer light or from a broader perspective—he or she assumes responsibility. This is a fact which I have consistently stressed during the last forty years, particularly at the beginning of my book, *The Practice of Astrology.** Anyone who reveals to another person a truth, a law, or any kind of knowledge, especially when that person will most likely be unable or unwilling to apply the knowledge in a constructive way or will use it destructively, incurs a perhaps grave responsibility. It may be that in the long run the person may nevertheless benefit from the knowledge or guidance, and that the first adverse reaction was unavoidable and made valuable by the ultimate results; but this does not lessen the responsibility of the teacher or guide.

Accepting responsibility for whatever one says or does in any form of interpersonal relationship is one of the basic prerogatives of being human. Man's destiny—and his burden—is to deliberately induce change in the processes of life and spiritual unfoldment, and he must accept responsibility for the changes. Refusing to change or to help make changes does not excuse one from taking responsibility either, for if an astrologer understands what the transpersonal process implies but refuses to assume that responsibility toward a client in need of transpersonal guidance, the astrologer may still be accountable for his or her 'non-action'—perhaps for the loss of the only chance the client had at that time to relate to a higher level of existence.

The only way an individual can in a sense transcend this responsibility is by having truly become an 'agent' for a transpersonal purpose and operation. But one can easily make oneself believe that one has actually become such an agent, while in reality what one says or does is entirely or mainly the product of one's personal self—a self which can wear many subtle disguises and whose mind can perform wonders of rationalization!

## The Birth-Chart as a Symbol of Individual Karma

A birth-chart calculated for the precise time and place of the first breath of a human organism is *the foundation* of a transpersonal as well as a person-centered interpretation. It represents what a human organism—which has the possibilities of becoming first a 'person', part of an organized community (sociocultural level), then an

---

*Now in its third edition, from Shambhala Publications (Boulder: 1978).

'individual' emerging as a self-actualizing, autonomous 'I', and last, of growing beyond this state of strictly individual selfhood—*starts from.*

The birth-chart refers to all that *conditions* the possibility of a human being's growth. But by saying 'conditions,' I do not mean 'determines.' Conditioning refers to a base from which one can operate in any direction; the character of this base conditions what one *is* as one proceeds, but it does not determine what one will *do* and, still less, *think.* For instance, the fact of being born as a member of a minority group in a city tenement indicates in social terms what the person starts from, and this 'conditions' the nature of the person's experiences in childhood and youth; yet it does not 'determine' whether he or she will become a heroin addict or the executive of some important business firm—both possibilities are there. The birth-chart of many an artistic or literary genius is often very similar to that of a psychotic in a mental institution.

Objectively understood, what we see in a birth-chart is the state which the solar system, viewed from the Earth, has reached at a particular moment. This state is a composite of the cyclic motions of all the planets, including the rotating motion of our globe around its axis. This birth-chart is a 'snapshot' of an immense continuum of activity in which all the planets, the Sun, Moon, and stars participate. We seem to have arrested that complex motion when we take a picture of it with our 'astrological camera', the birth-chart; but, in fact, the cyclic movements keep on going, each according to its own rhythms. The patterns produced by the relationship between any two or three of the moving celestial bodies will keep repeating themselves, as they have in the past. But they interact with other patterns in always new ways, unless we postulate a definitely limited universe.

The birth-chart is thus *not* a static picture drawn by a cosmic architect imagining fanciful buildings. This is why to speak of a birth-chart as the 'blueprint' of personality, while it is a convenient and at a certain level valuable simile (I have used it extensively myself), it is nevertheless not really an accurate statement of fact.

If we focus our attention on the personality of an individual and try to discover what we can expect of it as a whole at a particular time and in order to satisfy a particular interest or purpose, we can assume that it has a somewhat monolithic 'character'. But in fact a person is not a static entity that can be isolated from the forever moving universe—as for instance a statue. A human being is a small area of space in the midst of the immense wave which is the evolution of mankind. It is an area into which a vast number of ancestral currents of—we may want to assume psychic, mental, and spiritual forces that, when seen in their interrelated state, we call 'past incarnations' —*converge.*

Every human being is the convergence of a multitude of dynamic currents of energy and memories unrecognized, yet latent, and susceptible of being revived. The past of a countless number of atoms, of genetic patterns always seeking to repeat themselves, so great is their inertia, of cultural endeavors, and discoveries that have generated currents of energy as yet unexpanded—and, if one believes in *individual* reincarnation, of spiritual decisions which created either fulfillment in success or failure: all of this past acts in a new combination at the moment of birth. Every human life is, I repeat, but a brief moment in the total evolution of mankind—a drop of water within an immense wave, rising or breaking. When a baby is born, this evolution does not stop; the planets do not cease revolving around the Sun, nor does the Earth stop rotating around its polar axis. Because all these motions have inertia, every present moment in a dynamic process is founded upon a never-entirely-ended past. But every present moment, because of the same inertia, also contains a future in potentiality.

The realization of this fact has given rise to the concept of causality: every event has causes and will be the cause of future effects. This is also the basis of the Hindu concept of *karma,* which has become greatly materialized and emotionalized in India as well as in America. As the birth-chart symbolizes what the past of a particular evolutionary strand in the total evolution of mankind has led to, the birth-chart can therefore be considered to represent the karma of the newborn. This newborn is the result of millions of causes which, when considered together constitute his or her karma; and, being dynamic currents of energy, these causes will produce effects. What so many people fail to realize is that we can give different interpretations to the fact that all these currents have converged to form a particular human being.

When interpreted in a materialistic sense, the principle of causality leads to determinism. It has thus been said that if all the causes operating in the past were known, their effects, and even the future effects of these effects acting as causes, could also be totally known. Causality leads to the concept of predetermination. The fallacy of such an idea is that it considers the operation of forces *only* at one level—the physical level. It is fashionable today to speak of this type of thinking as 'linear' thinking. From my point of view, which I expressed in my book, *The Planetarization of Consciousness**, it concerns itself with only what are called 'horizontal' relationships—the relationship between entities operating at the same level of activity and consciousness.

The relationship of a newborn to his ancestors is a horizontal relationship, because it links in a linear sequence entities operating at the same biological level. Similarly, if by reincarnation one means the successive reappearances of the same entity, and one does not take into consideration any other factors except this entity periodically passing from the state of consciousness in a physical body to that of consciousness in a 'body' made of non-physical substance, this too refers to the 'horizontal' type of relationships between a series of incarnations, each one being the effect of previous causes (karma), and becoming the cause of future lives—i.e., generating new karma.

---

*ASI Publications, Inc.; New York, 1977.

The situation takes on a different aspect if we use the principle of holarchy as a basis for our interpretation of causality and karma. We then have to consider not only the relationships between entities operating at the same level, but the interaction between greater Whole and lesser wholes—that is, between entities operating at different levels. One can call the latter type of relationship 'vertical', though it is actually quite an unfortunate, even if convenient term. This so-called vertical type of relationship is rather one of *encompassment*: the greater Whole encompasses all the lesser wholes participating in it.

If one understands the implications of this concept, the whole picture of the world-process and of the possibilities inherent in the state of individual existence radically changes. The cause-and-effect principle working in 'horizontal' sequences and karmic relationships is not in any way negated, but it is seen to refer to *only one type* of relationships. The 'vertical' type introduces into human existence—and into the operations of all that exists in the universe—a new factor in the light of which many things that have so long appeared mysterious and miraculous can be interpreted in a simple and at least potentially understandable manner. For vertical relationships refer to the direct influence or impact (perhaps the 'blessing' or healing power), of a greater Whole upon the lesser whole —thus of Humanity (as the planetary Being), or of some 'divine Hierarchy' upon men and women in need of help or inspiration.

This directly applies to the transpersonal interpretation of an astrological birth-chart, because in light of it what is seen in the chart can be given a new meaning. The picture presented by the chart is still understood to represent the starting point of the individual. It depicts the convergence (and indeed focusing) of past cycles of activity into a new human being, thus his or her karma. But it can also have another meaning. It can be seen to represent the meaning and purpose with which the greater Whole, Humanity, has invested this birth—thus the *dharma* of the new human being.

## The Transmutation of Karma into Dharma

The term dharma simply defines what this new human being *could* do for Humanity of which he or she is a part, what Humanity expects of this individual, and what it will help him or her to do, if help is possible. Considered from the point of view of *karma*, the new birth is the result of a multitude of past causes and of the inertial power of the energy these causes generated; but from the point of view of *dharma*, the new birth constitutes a potential answer to a need of the greater Whole, Humanity. It is only, however, a *potential* answer, for the inertial power of karma may force merely a repetition of old patterns. Such a repetition would be almost inevitable if there were no possibility of the greater Whole deliberately interacting with the lesser whole, the human being. But such an inter- action is possible in a *focalized and individualized sense* only if the human being first opens his or her conscious- ness to that possibility—which means to the belief in the real 'presence' of this encompassing greater Whole, or of what the Christian religion *interprets* as the presence of God (thus the title of a well-known Medieval manual of devotion, *The Practice of the Presence of God).** 

In other words, a human being can transform karma into dharma if he or she is able to fulfill the purpose with which Humanity invested him or her at birth. The trans- mutation of karma into dharma *is* the transpersonal way. Along that way, the inertia of the individual's past is being

---

*In Catholic mysticism, the greater Whole, when interpreted at a spiritual level, is the Mystical Body of Christ "in whom we live, move and have our being." This mystical body is not only symbolized, but believed to be substantially present in the consecrated host. During the year for a specified time, every church exposes the host high above the altar in a golden container made in the symbolical shape of the Sun with radiating rays. This is the ritual of the 'perpetual Adoration'. At every moment in one or several churches around the globe, this ritual is being performed to symbolize the constant and encompassing Presence of Christ. The *circular* host is of course the symbol of divine perfection—the supreme mandala.

*used* to fulfill a need of humanity. As he or she struggles along the transpersonal way, the individual has to repolarize the energies and faculties from his or her past. The individual was born as the convergence of these energies and faculties, but it is possible for him or her to cease acting and thinking as a creature of the past and to become the creator of a future—or rather to become a focusing agent *through whom* Humanity (or the planetary Being, or God), is able to fulfill a particular and limited purpose. Such a repolarization is truly the essence of the transpersonal process.

The fallacy inherent in the ideal of personality fulfillment is the notion that what is fulfilled is something of the individual himself or herself. What is fulfilled is in fact the flowering of the past. In this sense, many great poets, artists, or thinkers can be considered the flowering of their cultures; and this is truly the ideal one works for at the sociocultural level of consciousness and activity. But the real 'genius', while in a sense the product of his or her culture, is nevertheless a flower that contains a mutating seed, a transformative agent. Most often, however, the 'genius' is not clearly conscious of being such an agent, because the I-center is still involved in the karmic patterns of the past. Even if there is a conscious realization of being a channel for some superior Power, the interpretation given to this fact may be as confusing as helpful.

The transpersonal way does not particularly deal with individuals belonging to the special category of 'genius'. It is open to all individuals who, because they inwardly feel, realize, or experience their relationship with a greater Whole (whether they interpret this relationship in religious, metaphysical or occult terms), are able to give a larger frame of reference to the conscious or half-conscious process of repolarizing what in them represents the past into a future that includes far more than their personality. In fact, the past of an individual is not merely the legacy of his or her biological ancestors and the mental-emotional accumulation of all that his or her culture has impressed upon him or her; it is also the unfinished business and failures of past personalities with whom the individual is psychically related and of the societies in which these personalities lived. The popular concept of reincarnation refers at best to *only one kind* of psychic relationship with personalities of the past, and it does not take into consideration group or national karma.

Astrologically speaking, all this past, however it is interpreted in a psychic or spiritual sense, is seen to be *condensed* in the birth-chart. More accurately, *the birth-chart as a whole* symbolizes what part of this immense past is condensed as the karma of the newborn human being—thus what has *conditioned* the new birth. No particular factor—planet, node, or house—can be especially related to the karma of the person. The entire chart—and in concrete terms, the family and environment (physical, mental, and social) of the newborn—represents his or her karma. This karma can be repolarized and transmuted into dharma, and the function of transpersonal astrology is to help individuals who not only consider such a repolarization possible, but are sincerely willing and seemingly ready (or at least very eager) to take some definite steps along this path of radical transformation.

A transpersonal interpretation of astrological data should first of all assist the individual in realizing how the energies of his or her whole person, the circumstances and major events of his or her life, can be given a new and transformative meaning. The purpose of the transpersonal interpretation is not to *describe* what the birth-chart may be said to indicate. It is to *evoke* the possibility of repolarizing what the past had produced into the means required for the performance of the future-oriented dharma, and to evoke this possibility in such a convincing manner that the individual will be stirred into taking active steps toward such a performance.

In order to accomplish this purpose, two procedures have to be used. First, every factor in the *birth-chart* must be interpreted in the light of the process of transformation, thus of what each can contribute to it. In order to do this so that the client will be able to understand and especially to assimilate and constructively respond to the interpretation (as I have already stated and cannot stress enough), the astrologer has to discover where the client stands in his or her evolution. This can be done to a large extent intuitively as well as by closely observing the behavior, mannerisms, and vocal inflexions of the client, especially when two alternative courses of action or inter-pretations are presented to him or her. At a strictly astrological level, the other procedure which is required is a careful and complete study of planetary *progressions and transits.*

These two factors represent the dynamic aspect of astrology, and for this reason they acquire a paramount value in transpersonal astrology; for transpersonal astrology essentially deals with *a process,* and not merely with a supposedly static entity whose identity is set at birth and outlined by an unchanging birth-chart. While a person-centered type of astrology seeks to discover the character of this identity and to help the fulfillment of the potentialities it reveals, transpersonal astrology deals mainly with the possibility of *using* whatever the birth-chart indicates to transform the very concept of individual identity *by raising the level at which it operates*— eventu-ally raising it from the 'I' level to that of a transindividual 'We'. This is the level of conscious and responsible par-ticipation in the greater Whole, Humanity, considered as a planetary Being.

*Transpersonal astrology* deals with a *dynamic process. The birth-chart* reveals its *starting point.* The process can be followed by the astrologer as it unfolds day by day, year by year. It can be 'tracked' in two ways because it has a twofold character. On one hand, it refers to a particular individual, but on the other, this person does not grow in a vacuum. The process of individual transformation occurs in a universe also in transformation and, more particular-ly, in a society and community undergoing constant changes. In our century these changes are so rapid, so violent, and so extensive that virtually no one's life can escape their direct or indirect impact.

As a result, astrology in its dynamic aspect uses two different techniques. The technique of *progressions* (secondary or 'solar') refers to the *individual* aspect of the process of transformation, while the study of *transits* (particularly those of the planets from Jupiter outwards) deals more specifically with the *collective* aspect of the change. The qualificative collective, however, should be applied to *both* the 'lower' collectivity constituted by a particular sociocultural environment, and to the 'higher' collectivity represented by the greater whole, Humanity, seeking to induce a conscious and open response in the individuals who participate in its planetary existence.

Before proceeding to study these dynamic aspects of astrology, we should first focus on the birth-chart at the transpersonal level.

# 7

## INTERPRETING THE BIRTH-CHART AT THE TRANSPERSONAL LEVEL

While transpersonal astrology deals primarily with a dynamic process of transformation, the birth-chart, I repeat, is the *starting point* of that process. It is like a seed which will develop into a full-grown tree, but in the case of a human being, this 'tree' has within itself the potentiality of becoming such a transparent structure that *through it* the glowing form of a *deva* (nature-spirit or dryad) may be able to reveal itself and, by so doing, affect and 'spiritualize' the surrounding 'forest' of mankind. A deva is a personification of a particular current of life-energy, which in its primary nature is a differentiated aspect of solar energy. A human being is a particular aspect of Humanity-as-a-whole which, spiritually considered, is the planetary Being that encompasses all that exists within the field of activity and consciousness of Earth, Gaya.

Transpersonal astrology is essentially concerned with the possibility, inherent in every human newborn, of achieving a state of symbolic 'transparency' enabling the spiritual power that archetypal Man represents to radiate through him or her, and to do so consciously and as an individual form of selfhood. This possibility can be said to be inherent in the human seed (the fecundated ovum), yet its *actualization* depends entirely on the fact of being born as a baby *within a collective society with a particular culture*. Left alone on a desert island, the newborn would die, or if—as apparently has happened—a baby were to be adopted by an animal able and willing to provide milk and protection, the child would grow as an animal in whom no self-conscious mind could develop. Without such a mind, there is no actual and effective *humanhood*.

This is why the moment of birth (the first breath) is used in the practice of astrology rather than the difficult-to-ascertain moment of conception. An embryo is not 'human' in the strict sense of the term. One might say it is 'alive', just as a seed is alive—but a human being is not *merely* a living being. It is, in the broadest sense of the term, mind in the process of development—a process which may lead to individualization, and on the basis of individual selfhood, to a transindividual state of consciousness and activity.

This process of mental development is complex and at first totally conditioned by culture. The first phase of the process produces a personal psyche which results, on the one hand, from the passive acceptance of family and sociocultural values and goals and, on the other hand, from a self-assertive and rebellious drive for independence which is the central factor in the formation of an ego, as I have defined the term. At the individual level, the drive for independence becomes the center of the field of consciousness, the 'I'. But in the process of individualization, a polarization occurs; symbolically speaking, two 'areas' are formed in the total field of the personality—the field of consciousness centered in the 'I', and the soul.* The soul retains strong links with the 'lower collectivity' — the culture-whole and its collective assumptions and traditions—but it can also become a quiet lake upon which the presence of 'higher collectivity' will be able to reflect itself, generating in the whole personality exalting or disturbing feeling-intuitions through significant dreams or so-called 'peak-experiences'.

Whatever form the processes of personal growth and individualization take, they have a starting point and, as we have just seen, the birth-chart represents this 'first point' of human existence. The birth-chart, the positions

---

*Cf. my use of this term in Chapter 5.

of the planets and their complex geometrical relationships (astrological 'aspects') within the framework defined by the natal horizon and meridian, have to be studied. This study deals with the *static* aspect of astrology, whereas progressions and transits refer to its *dynamic and transformative* aspect. But even the apparently static features of a birth-chart can also be understood as a mere snapshot freezing an unceasing process of cosmic change within which planets, stars, and galaxies pursue their cyclic courses. No *absolute* beginning or end can be attributed to this process, yet human beings instinctively think of an at least relative beginning, the act of divine creation, as they project their experience of birth and death upon the universe.

The birth of a human being is the 'relative' beginning of a process which, from the transpersonal point of view, can have an illumined and translucent end. This end is conditioned, but not determined, by the birth-chart as a whole. In order to help an individual to work consciously toward such an end, the astrologer using a transpersonal approach should be able to see the planetary components of the birth-chart in a new light.

# A Transpersonal Interpretation of Sun, Moon and Planets

At the *biological* level of interpretation, we saw that the Sun symbolizes the principle of Fatherhood or the positive and fecundant aspect of the life-force. At the *sociocultural* level, the Sun represents the drive to social recognition, power, and prestige. It refers to the ambition to become a center of influence around which other persons will gravitate and revolve and thus (symbolically), a 'king' with more or less absolute power—that is, the unchecked ability to use the power and psychism engendered by the cooperation and psychomental integration of a more or less large number of other human beings, and that ability is colored by the specific character of a particular culture. When we reach the *individual* level, the symbol of kingship becomes introverted. The principle of individual selfhood operates at the center of the mandala of personality—where the natal horizon and meridian intersect—but the *actual operation* of that principle is to be related to the Sun. I have spoken of it as the individualized will; it is also the manifested purpose of the I-center seeking the fulfillment of the innate potentialities latent in the human being whose biopsychic energies it brings to a conscious focus.

At the *transpersonal* level, the Sun has an ambiguous meaning, because in actual astronomical fact the Sun is not only the source of the power that rules the solar system up to the orbit of Saturn and whose influence to some extent radiates beyond Saturn through the 'aura' of the system; it is also one of the billions of stars constituting our galaxy, the Milky Way.* The Sun in the chart of an individual on his or her way to a transindividual state should therefore symbolize a factor which links the individual to the transindividual level. Religious philosophers and moralists have spoken of the 'God within', Christ Immanuel—and in India, of the *jivatma*, the incarnated manifestation of the transcendent reality *atman*. Transpersonally interpreted, the position of the Sun in a birth-chart thus represents the individual quality of the will-to-be-related-to and participate in the activity and consciousness of a greater Whole. Theoretically this greater Whole is the planetary being of Humanity; but when the mind of the individual is as yet unable to deal with the implications of such a vast and global organism, it has to limit its image of the reality of a greater whole to the community or nation in which the individual operates, either by birthright or by individual choice.

This solar will to be related to a greater whole finds inspiration and sustainment in the Moon. I have already referred to the Moon as the 'soul',† and said that this soul represents, at least symbolically, an 'area' of the total human being which has developed in polar opposition to

---

*Cf. my previously mentioned book, *The Sun is Also a Star: The Galactic Dimension of Astrology* (New York: A.S.I. Publishers, 1975).

†Cf. Chapter 5.

the will to emerge from the sociocultural collectivity and become an autonomous individual—a will symbolized by the Sun during the process of individualization. This soul-area has—I repeat—remained related to the collective psychism of the culture-whole; it had to do so in order to develop its potential and future function as a complement or balance to the individual character of the increasingly authoritarian and powerful I-center. But while the soul is *rooted* in the culture (lower collectivity), it also develops the ability to respond to the downflow of energy and inspiration from the higher collectivity—the encompassing field of activity and consciousness of the greater Whole. The soul links the sociocultural collective to the transcendent reality of Humanity-as-a-whole which, in religious terms, is represented by the Mystical Body of Christ.

If we use the old Chinese terms, the soul is Yin, the individualized I-center, Yang. The soul is the "Eternal Feminine that draws men upwards," as Goethe states at the close of *Faust*. But if the soul fails in its function, 'she' takes the form of the 'femme fatale' who draws the individualized 'I' down and back to the lower collective, usually by re-energizing the biological drives of the masculine 'I', or by compelling him for her sake (and perhaps for the sake of children born of their relationship) to re-become a slave to the power of the culture, the institutionalized religious organization and/or the traditional patterns of society—thus a 'normal person' with the average citizen's standardized interests.

There are cases in which the spiritually ambitious, yet emotionally unready individual craving to 'storm the gates of heaven' needs to be made aware of how unready he or she really is. Then the 'feminine' soul may be compelled by karma to act as the Temptress (Kundry in Wagner's *Parsifal*). In this case, she is used by higher powers within the greater Whole to serve as a tester of the men she unwillingly attracts.

All processes of transition from a lower to a higher level generate what Carl Jung called the Shadow—a fact that Medieval theologians and Occultists expressed by saying that Satan is God inverted. Satan symbolizes an *inversion* of the transpersonal process—an inversion in most cases engendered by the pride of being able to develop an apparently totally independent, self-motivated individuality. Such a pride-intoxicated I-center eventually destroys the soul-area, and by so doing cuts itself loose from *both* the lower and the higher collectivity. It eventually becomes *a center without a circumference,* a mere abstract point, individuality pushed to the extreme in a quasi-absolute repudiation of the desire for relationship. This is the end of the inverted transpersonal process—the end in store for the 'black magician'. The 'white magician', on the other hand, is produced by the 'divine Marriage' of the objectively conscious and centered 'I' with the soul. This is the higher kind of alchemical Marriage which, as we already saw, must occur in the 'presence of God', that is, in a conscious relationship with the greater Whole, Humanity as a spiritual pleroma of beings.

The natal relationship of the Moon to the Sun in a person's chart has thus a profound transpersonal meaning, because it should tell us a great deal concerning the character which the possible union of 'I' and soul is likely to have, and its purpose—*if* it occurs at all, in even a partial manner. The aspect between the natal Sun and Moon, and the positions they occupy in the zodiacal signs and natal houses should evoke in the astrologer's mind the karmic foundation of this Sun-Moon (Yang-Yin) relationship. But *at the same time,* they should point to the best way—the way of destiny—in which the individual can use the solar and lunar functions. Though they have been developed in the ancestral and spiritual-reincarnational past, they can and should be used as incentives and tools when the individual begins to search for, and eventually to walk upon the transpersonal path.

The planet Mercury, in its highest aspect, is what Indian philosophers have called *budhi*—its supreme manifestation being the *Buddha-mind.* It is the mind of wisdom, the mind of the Sage who has transcended the conflicts and the dualism inherent in the intellect. In an objective and occult sense, one can see in such a mind a reflection of the consciousness of the greater Whole; and esoteric tradition states that Gautama the Buddha was the first human being whose consciousness was able freely to soar beyond the boundaries of the solar system into galactic space.

In a transpersonally interpreted natal chart Mercury represents the best manner in which the sociocultural mind inherited at birth by a human being can be reoriented, repolarized, and eventually transmuted into a 'calm lake' able to reflect the most distant 'stars'. The atmosphere above the 'lake' should be pure, unpolluted and frosty-clear—the 'frost' referring here to a mentality that has transcended the 'warmth' of human emotions and glamorous devotional feelings, a mentality able to operate in terms of the cool, superpersonal quality of cosmic principles and relationships.

The planet Venus should be understood to refer essentially to the capacity to pass judgments on the worth of whatever one encounters. At the *biological* level, value is appreciated in organismic terms: what is met will either foster the development of, and bring well-being to, the body and its functional activies, or it will hinder and impair them. At the *sociocultural* level, the members of a collectivity pass value-judgments according to shared moral standards. Love and hate, embrace or flight, cultural and esthetical enjoyment, or critical and emotional repudiation all have a collective foundation which is but partially modified or superficially colored by personal idiosyncrasies.

At the level of a dynamic type of *individualization*, Venus acquires an individualized power of creativity. But at this level, creativity mostly means a projection of the individual's I-center and its autonomous characteristics onto materials made available by the culture from which the 'I' has to some extent been able to emerge. The 'I' uses the cultural materials for its own purpose—the ideal of self-fulfillment and often merely of self-glorification.

At the *transpersonal* level, Venus can be interpreted as the capacity to give individual forms to spiritual ideals which have, as it were, seeped into the field of consciousness, either through the calmed and assuaged mind, or through the soul acting as a channel for the descent of 'galactic' forces. Nevertheless, the early value system impressed upon the growing personality through childhood and adolescence undoubtedly has in most instances valuable features which should be retained. Similarly, the psychic and mental harvest of one's ancestral culture can be used on the transpersonal path to suggest valid lines of approach to the problems of developing *discrimination*—a crucially needed quality when an individual is faced by options from which he or she has to choose.

Venus, in another sense, is the *archetypal form* of the individuality. It may seem that this form has to be transcended on the transpersonal way, but what has to be transcended is actually not the individual form itself; rather, it is the *personal attachment* to its perpetuation as an isolated and supposedly self-sufficient entity. In other words, the essential character (or archetypal form) of the 'I' is not negated or destroyed. What happens is that the 'galactic We'—the pleroma state of consciousness—is allowed by the individual to focus itself in a particular way through his or her 'I' in order to fulfill a particular human or planetary need. But within the 'We', the 'I' remains what it archetypally is. It remains, however, in a transfigured condition; the 'form' is retained, but the 'contents' of the form are transsubstantiated.

The planet Mars is always to be understood as the capacity to mobilize energy, either in the pursuit of a goal which the Venus function has proclaimed desirable, or as a spontaneous release of an excess of energy having reached a nearly explosive state. *Biologically,* Mars is the muscle power and glandular stimulation needed to hunt and overcome physical obstacles, perform the sexual function or defeat enemies. In a *sociocultural* sense, Mars retains much the same character to which is added the ability to work for the fulfillment of a social or cultural ambition.

As the process of *individualization* pursues its course, Mars takes on a more differentiated character of self-assertion. It can become the power to achieve a successful but egocentric rebellion against the sociocultural norm and the religious-moral tradition, or it can transform itself into an intense devotion for an ideal cause or to a guru.

In its *transpersonal* aspect, Mars is the introverted power that steels the ascetic will of the individual trying to rush along the path, but who is perhaps only headed toward a precipice or an encounter with foes that can hardly be overcome. At all levels, Mars should always work *with* Venus, but especially so on the transpersonal path when Venus takes the form of discrimination. If surrounded by the typically transformative planets (Uranus, Neptune and Pluto), the 'red planet' may become a hostage to forces over which the individual has little control, but through such experiences it may also become the servant of transindividual forces emanating from the greater Whole, Humanity.

Jupiter and Saturn are characteristically the 'social' planets in the sense that they refer respectively to personal *expansion* derived from human togetherness and cooperation, and to the *security* gained from participating in and being protected by an organized community. Expansion and security have first biological, then social aspects. At the individual level, Jupiter often represents the inner pride of the individual who feels superior to the mass of non-individualized persons in bondage to collective values and institutions—thus the feeling of belonging to an elite. In some 'esoteric' groups, this may be the often patronizing feeling of being an 'old soul' in the midst of as yet 'young' souls. Saturn may well crystallize this sense of superiority by establishing group-patterns that rigidly define a hierarchical structure affecting all interpersonal relationships.

Thus, these two planets can act in a more or less subtly negative manner when the ideal of a transpersonal path begins to permeate the collective consciousness of the most progressive members of a culture-whole. To tread this transpersonal path without a deep sense of humility and compassion (to which Neptune often refers) and without a mind free from dogmatism and reliance upon narrow principles of structural organization (a freedom that Pluto may provide) can indeed be very dangerous. Uncontrolled Mars-represented energy, polluted by the fashions of a chaotic society and a degenerating culture, can also add more fire to pride and dogmatism; and the Mercury mind, turned into a rationalizing mechanism to give support to a massive and intractable I-center, can also play a very negative role.

The basic issue is whether the individual 'I', having become aware of the existence of a level of collective being transcending the sociocultural level, can only think of reaching that higher state by still using his or her newly individualized powers according to the collective concepts and patterns of activity of his or her culture-whole—or if he or she realizes that one can only contact the higher collectivity by repudiating what essentially belongs to the lower collective (the culture and the social way of life). Repudiation does not mean total isolation, although a *temporary* period of isolation, or inward withdrawal and denudation, often seems to be necessary.

Whatever is necessary—and this may mean a crucial crisis or total upheaval in the personal life or in the society in which one is active—can be attributed to Uranus, Neptune, and Pluto acting as 'agents' for the galaxy. These transformative planets may operate in a great variety of ways. They often operate *through* a particular type of individuals who (whether they want to or not, and often against their conscious intentions) relate to men and women who are at least partially ready to embark on the transpersonal voyage across storm-ridden seas and act as arousing or even deeply disturbing factors.

As I have stated elsewhere,* each of the trans-Saturnian planets acting as an agent (or 'ambassador') of the galactic greater Whole (which, I repeat, symbolizes Humanity as a planetary Being), is particularly meant to disturb and transform one of the other planets. Uranus seeks to break through the fortified walls Saturn has built to give maximum security to the reign of the kingly 'I', and to bring a new perspective and a breath of 'fresh air'. Neptune is especially adept at dissolving Jupiterian pride and pomposity. And Pluto can act most effectively as a purifier of Martian emotional drives. As a cathartic agent, Pluto seeks to remove from the personality (which has become individualized through often devious means generating heavy karmic 'toxins'), whatever does not strictly belong to the archetypal character of the emergent individuality—and Pluto's action can be drastic and

---

*Cf. *The Sun is Also a Star, (The Galactic Dimension of Astrology)*

relentless. But Pluto in its cosmic aspect can also reveal to the purified, but probably rudely shaken individual the true archetypal form of his or her individual selfhood and/or destiny.

At the transpersonal level, Uranus, the iconoclast, deals with the image of the 'enthroned I' and its 'courtiers' bowing to its every desire. It tries to show the mind how actually ineffective, ridiculous, or empty of meaning this image really is. During the seven years of its passage through a zodiacal sign, Uranus tends to either discredit, deeply disturb, or challenge the traditional character or meaning of the mode of activity represented by that sign—at times in a direct manner, at others by forcing repeated experiences of this mode of activity and its by-products upon the consciousness, until the 'king-I' is satiated or disgusted.

The natal house in which Uranus is located in most cases points to the type or field of experience where the iconoclastic and revolutionary impact of the planet is most effective or most likely to operate. For instance, in terms of the transpersonal process, Uranus in the 12th house evokes the possibility that the individual's ability to act as a transforming agent will be in some manner closely related to a public crisis or to the process of transformation of society or some aspect of its culture. On the other hand, Uranus in the 6th house suggests a more personal kind of transformative upheaval and the need for a special type of service, perhaps of total surrender to a cause or guru.

In any house, a planet can be transpersonally interpreted as a message conveyed through the soul to the I-center open to the reception of such communication from 'above'—or released by the mind having realized that it can reflect a transcendent kind of consciousness—a message suggesting how the field of experience symbolized by the house should be reoriented.

Neptune, the universal Solvent, in many but obviously not all cases, tends to lower the effectiveness of the biological energies operating in the part of the body related to the zodiacal sign in which it is located. It throws doubt upon the validity of what the individual's community or nation considers valuable in the field of sociocultural activity and everyday living associated with the sign. According to the house in which it is located, it often brings deep confusion and a sense of futility that no rational explanation can quite dissipate. Yet Neptune can inspire compassion and the desire to participate in large and impersonal organizations. It universalizes and perhaps unfocuses the type of experiences related to the natal house through which it slowly moves after birth. This is particularly the case when found at one of the four Angles.

Pluto, the cathartic agent clearing from any field of activity the unnecessary or decaying material that has accumulated in it, can be seen at work in mankind as a whole as it passes slowly from one zodiacal sign to the next. While in Gemini (1884 to 1912-13), it revealed how superficial and incomplete were the intellectual pictures physical and psychological scientists had drawn during the century of triumphant materialism. As it became a publicly known fact of existence while transiting the sign Cancer (1913-1938), it produced an intense upheaval in the ideal of the family, and it gnawed at the roots of the concept of the classical, monolithic, and morally responsible individual personality through depth-psychology and the popularization of technological gadgets expected to solve personal problems at least in routine matters of everyday living—which inevitably leads to a subtle kind of automatism. In the name of the need for law and order, it produced—as an answer to the fear of the unknown—the negative and obsolete concepts of Fascism in politics and neo-classicism in the arts. To the new craving for the abundant life, it answered with the great Depression, and to a mechanical approach to world-organization and the hegemony of the victorious powers of World War I, it answered with the Nazi armored-divisions and Hitler's biological paranoia and political pride.

The character which Pluto's entrance into Leo took had been conditioned by the way mankind had responded to the planet's passage through Cancer. What had been issues basically concerning new and larger schemes of organization and the release of forces uprooting the *collective* past became issues more specifically aimed at the way *individuals* were made to experience and give value to their lives. These lives were now increasingly controlled by technology and technocrats (from medical doctors and psychologists to politicians and business specialists), by the media and by the result of a new general acquaintance (through movies, radio, air travel, and later TV) with all the countries and cultures of the world.

At first this was revolutionizing and often intoxicating —in different ways, depending on whether one belonged to a victorious or vanquished country, to the Communist or 'Free' World. But as Pluto entered Virgo in 1957 and later (1965-66) was joined by Uranus, the sense of global crisis began to pervade the new generations; they rose in protest, intoxicated by rather naive hopes and Utopian dreams. Virgo is a sign of transformation based on the criticism of what one has come to feel subjected to, whether be it as a result of one's previous actions or of what the preceding generations have built.

We have not yet seen the full effect of the passage of Pluto through Libra (1971 to 1984), nor can we estimate what challenges it may bring to individuals who will have to face in childhood or adolescence the possibility of crucial world-events as Pluto passes through Scorpio and comes *closer to the Sun than Neptune*, while making a 90-year long sextile aspect to this planet (1943-2038).

This penetration of Neptune's orbit by Pluto—I have spoken of it as a cosmic fecundation or impregnation—occurs approximately every 248 years. It occurred during the 18th century and what has become known as 'the Enlightenment' period which saw the rise of modern science and industry, the American War of Independence and the French Revolution. It led, in Europe, to the Napoleonic concept of a totally centralized bureaucracy and to a violent political reaction after the Emperor's downfall. An era of popular revolution and the spread of Romanticism followed, and modern individualism arose on the foundation of the power of bourgeoisie and of business—a foundation based on greed and productivity at any cost.

Mankind, of course, has to deal with all the direct and indirect results of these 19th century developments. It has to deal with them collectively at both the sociocultural and (through pollution and impaired health) the biological levels. This, under present circumstances, inevitably means some kind of world-crisis. If I have repeatedly mentioned this fact, it is because I must stress that the possibility and the character of radical *individual* transformation is largely conditioned by the crises through which our *society and today mankind as a whole* are passing. Individual transformation *does not occur in a vacuum.*

If, in this year 1978, I am writing a book on an astrological approach to the problems arising from the process of transformation of individuals or would-be individuals, it is because Pluto in Libra, Neptune in Sagittarius, and Uranus in Scorpio (more or less at the midpoint of the long Pluto-Neptune sextile, exact on the day I started this chapter), represent the possibility for my consciousness to tune up in a particular way to the downflow of new creative impulses that seek to renew, individually and collectively, the still prevailing patterns and ideals of human living. Many individuals evidently do now respond, and have responded, to such a release of transformative energy; each responds in his or her own individual way. But all these transformative concepts and formulations are individual interpretations of *the reflections* cast upon the minds of the transforming agents by the descent of spiritual forces emanating from the greater Whole, Humanity—astrologically symbolized by the galaxy—in answer to the developing needs of nations, communities, and individual persons. Their need 'rises to heaven,' as it were, as an unconscious (or in some cases conscious) prayer; the answer 'descends' from one aspect or another of the planetary Mind—the pleroma Mind—in order to evoke the possibility of a radical change of consciousness and of our everyday approach to personal living and interpersonal relationship.

## Planetary Interactions: Aspects and Gestalt

Whether one thinks of a birth-chart as the blueprint of a 'building' or as a mandala symbolizing the complex interplay of energies within an I-centered personality, it is a geometrical figure. It is conveniently as well as signifi-

cantly divided into four sections by the cross of horizon
and meridian. The planets—and any other celestial factors
used in astrology—are located in these four sections, and
if their positions are interrelated by lines, a geometric
pattern (or *gestalt*) becomes visible.

In order really to understand the implications of a birth-
chart, it has to be perceived and interpreted as a whole.
This is as true at the transpersonal level as at the person-
centered level of interpretation. The only difference is the
the end-purpose of the interpretation. In my book, *Person-
Centered Astrology*,* I have dealt at some length with what
I called the 'planetary gestalt' of the chart, that is, with the
specific way planets are grouped, especially with regard
to the horizon and meridian axes. I shall not repeat here
what I have written in other books, but will only add that
these planetary patterns, when they are quite clear-cut
(which is not always the case), provide the astrologer with
a basic frame of reference within which he or she can
evaluate repeating patterns of activities and of events.

To illustrate what I mean by the difference between a
person-centered and transpersonal interpretation of
overall planetary pattern (*gestalt*), let us take for example a
pattern in which a grouping of planets in one hemisphere
of the chart (or one of the four main quadrants) broadly
opposes one planet, or two or three in close proximity.
From the person-centered point of view, what is shown by
such a type of formation is the need for establishing a
stable balance between the two sets of planets—or if
possible the integration of presumably conflicting
tendencies into a 'fulfilled' personality. From the transpersonal point of view, such a dualistic pattern is not
something to *overcome*, but rather something to be
consciously *used*. What is to be used for the process of
transformation is the tension between the two groups of
planets.

There may be tensions of another kind when an empty
hemisphere (180°) contrasts with one containing all the
planets; these may also be condensed within a smaller
space. In such cases, the section where the planets are
congregated symbolizes an 'area' of the total personality

---

*Cf. the chapter entitled "First Steps in the Study of Birth-Charts."

to which, in this particular life, much attention (literally, 'tension toward') should be directed. Life itself will presumably *force* the person's attention to that area, but the real issue is whether this 'attention' will be compulsive —as in the case of serious illness or of a repetitive pattern of frustrating or tragic interpersonal relationships—and leave the person as unaware as before of the *inherent transformative purpose* of the events, or whether the individual will be able to meet these happenings as tools for the cutting and grinding of the coarse and dull stone of personality into a clear and translucent jewel.

This is why the often repeated statement that we must 'live in the now' is only partially right and may blind its advocates to the higher possibilities of human existence. The now—the present moment—is only a transition between past and future. Most people live their lives in such a way that the present is always, not only conditioned, but often entirely determined by the past—and this is unfortunate and rather meaningless. An individual on the transpersonal path should realize in what way a present occurrence is an *effect* of the past, and at the same time, understand the *purpose* of the event in generating power to move *ahead* in the process of transformation. This does *not* mean that one should make definite pictures of the future in one's mind—far from it. It means that a future-oriented energy should be released from any present happening (whatever it be, 'good' or 'bad', pleasurable or disturbing).

This of course runs counter to the modern gospel of enjoyment or 'instant satisfaction' in terms of strictly personal feelings and moods and regardless of possible future consequences or by-products. But our modern age is mostly hedonistic, and the search for pleasure within a strictly personal and egocentric frame of reference negates the possibility of any real advance on the transpersonal way. This, however, is not to be considered a glorification of asceticism, for ascetic practices are often undertaken for a personal or strictly individual purpose disguised as 'spirituality'. What counts is not what is done or not done, but the spirit in which the action or refusal to act is performed.

I shall repeat here what during the last 50 years I have

so often stated in articles, lectures, and books: there is no 'good' or 'bad' birth-chart—no chart is 'better' than any other—no aspect between planets, and no planetary position in any zodiacal sign or natal house is in itself 'fortunate' or 'unfortunate' according to a common standard of value applicable to all human beings. Some charts apparently display a number of aspects which would indicate a relatively smooth, harmonious kind of relationship between the planets involved. These may actually represent obstacles to the process of transformation, because they may suggest an inertial kind of satisfaction with what is.

On the other hand, other charts may seem to portend what we would consider lasting difficulties, frustrations, and misfortunes from a biological or social point of view. But from the point of view of what the person was meant to accomplish—his or her dharma—these difficulties, tensions, and even apparent tragedies may be, and ought to be interpreted as, indispensable phases of the life-process. What takes the form of 'discordant' relationships between planets has the potentiality of generating power; and if this power can be controlled, or even objectively understood and accepted for what it is, it can increase the momentum of the process of transformation. In trans-personal living, an individual should not be concerned with 'success' and especially with what from the socio-cultural point of view would be called a constructive achievement. It may be that as far as all appearances reveal, a person does not end his or her life in an at least relative state of serenity or 'holiness,' or as an agent for transindividual and 'divine' purposes; nevertheless he or she may have neutralized a prolonged karma of failure—and thus a 'dark' spot on the total planetary being, Humanity. For karma is not, I repeat, merely an individual matter: every individual failure—and also every individual victory over the inertia of the past—affects the whole of mankind. And the life of an individual on the trans-personal way is totally involved in the evolution of humanity.

I might add here that when an individual decides to start

a course of action, which according to his or her nature cannot be easy and pleasurable because the person is bound to face strong opposition (either within the body and psyche, or in the social collectivity in whose midst the actions are performed), the process should best be started under interplanetary aspects which suggest a strong release of power—for instance under a square or a conjunction involving dynamic planets. Power is released out of a state of tension: a loosely stretched violin string does not produce a resonant tone! But it is also obvious that if the string is too taut it could break.

The series of astrological aspects which refer particularly to the release of power through tension are the squares and semi-squares, and the conjunctions in which at least one dynamic and potentially transformative planet is involved. Mars at the biological and emotional levels, and Uranus at the transpersonal level, are the most change-producing planets.

An opposition between two planets evokes the existence of a basic need for *objectively* seeing the meaning of the relationship between the biopsychic functions these planets symbolize; and this involves a clear and conscious differentiation between the purposes of these functions in the total personality. For example, at Full Moon the Sun and Moon are in opposition. This enables us to see the relation between these two 'Lights'—the Light of Day (activity directed by the conscious mind and the ego or the I-center's will) and the Light of Night (activity which, in a natural state of life, refers to interpersonal relationships in the home or at public places, procreation perhaps, and the dream state in which the feelings and experiences of the day may be given either chaotic or symbolic forms).

An opposition aspect is the apex of a cycle defined by the successive conjunctions of two planets. In the case of the 30-day lunation cycle, the cycle begins at New Moon, reaches its apex at Full Moon, and ends as the waning Crescent (or rather 'decrescent') disappears from the sky. This lunation cycle is the prototype of all cycles of relationship between two planets moving at different speeds, and I have dealt with it at great length in my book *The Lunation Cycle.** 

The Part of Fortune is the moving index of this cyclically evolving soli-lunar relationship. It is quite important in a transpersonal interpretation because at that level the location of the Part of Fortune in relation to the Angles of the birth-chart (its house position) symbolizes the concrete form which the relationship between the I-center and the soul may take, as the individual enters the path of transformation. For example, the Part of Fortune's conjunction with Saturn in the natal chart evokes karmic delays and psychic or social difficulties on the transpersonal way, difficulties often colored by the character of the zodiacal sign in which it is located. Such delays or difficulties, while they may retard the transpersonal process in time, can nevertheless bring greater depth to the relationship between the I-center and the soul. On the other hand, the Part of Fortune's conjunction with Jupiter in the birth-chart may facilitate the process of transformation through contacts with an authoritative personage. But Jupiter's social character can also unfocus the transpersonal search by bringing it back to the level of social success and wealth-seeking.

Every geometrically measured angular aspect between two moving planets is actually a phase—frozen and out of context, as it were—of a cyclic process extending from one conjunction of two planets to the next. Therefore, the interpretation of the aspect should in many cases take into consideration the sign and degree of the zodiac and the natal house in which the conjunction of the two planets occurred in the past. Moreover, I have insisted for many

---

*The *Lunation Cycle* was first published by the McKay firm (1946) under the erroneous title "The Moon: The Parts and Fortunes of Life" when Marc Jones was the editor in charge of astrological and occult publications. After this department was unexpectedly closed, the book, considerably expanded, was published by Servire Publications in Holland (1967), and is now in paperback by Shambhala Publications in Boulder, Colorado (1971). The Part of Fortune and its complements are also studied in this book.

There is also a large chapter concerning aspects in my already-mentioned book, *Person-Centered Astrology,* "Form in Astrological Time and Space" (New York: A.S.I. Publishers)

years upon the fact that an aspect occurring between the conjunction and opposition of a cycle of relationship between two planets has a meaning basically different from the one it would have found between the opposition and the next conjunction. In other words, a First Quarter of the cycle of soli-lunar relationships means in principle something very different from a Last Quarter phase. This can be seen concretely in the sky, because the two Quarter Moons, though having the same shape, face opposite directions; and the same phenomenon can be seen through a telescope with regard to the phases of Venus and other planets. *Geometrically* and in a static sense, the two square aspects within one cycle are identical, but *dynamically* they have opposite polarities.

In many instances, this difference in polarity can be given a valuable transpersonal meaning, for a truly transpersonal interpretation is concerned with dynamic processes rather than with static, abstract forms; and by considering the polarity of a planetary aspect, the astrologer may have a significant clue as to the level at which the energy generated by the relationship can most usefully operate. A 'waxing' aspect deals more specifically with physical, emotional and personal activity, while a 'waning' aspect refers particularly to mental and sociocultural processes—and I use the terms waxing and waning symbolically, in the way they apply to the phases of the Moon which, I repeat, are actually phases in the *relationship* between the Moon and the Sun.

Such an interpretation is particularly significant when one is considering the relationship between two planets which can be considered a bipolar pair—thus Sun and Moon, Mars and Venus, Jupiter and Mercury, Jupiter and Saturn, Sun and Saturn, Moon and Saturn, Saturn and Uranus, Jupiter and Neptune, Mars and Pluto, Uranus and Pluto—and, in terms of the development of culture-wholes and nations, Neptune and Pluto. In the last-mentioned case, a waxing sextile—such as the one we are presently experiencing—is profoundly different from a waning sextile (the one near the end of the last Neptune-Pluto cycle having occurred about 1841-43). The present *waxing* sextile of Neptune and Pluto remains effective ('in orb') for nearly 90 years, while the last *waning* sextile lasted only a couple of years.*

## Angles: Root-factors in Personality and their Transformation

At whatever level one may study and apply it, astrology is based, not only on relationships, but on cycles of relationships. At one time for convenience sake I differentiated between cycles of position and cycles of relationship.† The former, I said, refers to the cycle defined by the return of a planet (or of any regularly moving factor) to a fixed point in the sky—for instance, the lunar cycle of 27⅓ days defined by the return of the Moon to a conjunction with a fixed star. But because of the 'precession of the equinoxes', stars are not 'fixed'. Everything in the universe is moving—and moving with reference to everything else. The transpersonal approach, not only to astrology, but to every mode of interpreting the human experience of unceasing change, is essentially a dynamic approach.

Yet human beings also experience stability and permanence, and the most precious feeling of permanence for most people is the feeling of being 'I, myself'—a feeling so precious that the sense of identity it produces has to be considered immortal and even in some metaphysics, absolutely indestructible. For many, if not most astrologers, this 'I'—as a 'spiritual entity'—is thought to be *outside* of the birth-chart, separate from and (theoretically) able to rule it. Yet, as I have stated, the 'I' of which a person is often so proud and wanting to immortalize is largely the product of biological and sociocultural conditions of life. It is the center of the mandala of personality, but that center could not actually exist without an existential framework that gives it not only

---

*Cf. my books *An Astrological Timing: The Transition to the New Age*, Chapter 3, "Cycles of Relationship," and *The Sun is Also a Star*, Chapter 6, "The Interpenetrating Cycles of Uranus, Neptune and Pluto."

†Cf. *The Lunation Cycle*, Chapter 1.

power but, even more fundamentally, concreteness. Such a framework is represented in person-centered astrology by the four Angles of the birth-chart.

I have spoken of the Angles as the 'roots of the individualized consciousness,' as 'the four characteristic types of activity which participate in the building and development of a conscious and stable center within the whole human being'. I have also characterized the Ascendant as 'the symbolic point of sunrise at which the 'I' can most effectively discover its purpose' and at which 'illumination' may be received.

The meanings I have already given to the four Angles are essentially retained in a transpersonal interpretation, because as long as the consciousness can be radically influenced by biological and chemical needs of pressures, the power of the 'roots' has effectively to sustain the process of transformation—until the possibility of existence at a transphysical level is definitely actualized, in which case astrology is no longer applicable. Astrology interprets *physically based events and developments,* even if they are called psychological, mental, or occult.

Astrology is of value at the transpersonal level because it can reveal the meaning of the sequence of events and crises *during the process* of transformation and thus assist the traveler on the Path to understand where he or she stands, and why certain problems and resistances have to be met. It is no longer of any value once the process is completed and the physical plane is left behind, unless perhaps the now-transphysical being centered in the 'star' returns in some manner to the ordinary world of merely human beings to pursue in a subliminal and presumably hidden way the line that had been his or her dharma as an individual person.

Wherever and whenever this dharma remains a motivating force, the four Angles which were the 'roots' that brought substantiality and earthly power to the 'I' retain their original character. But as the transpersonal process unfolds, what was the 'closed-center' mandala of personality should become an 'open-center' mandala. The central area of the mandala had previously been filled by the 'palace' of the I-centered consciousness and will. But what had once been the solid and majestic throne on which the power of individualized selfhood was glorified as the absolute reality of human existence becomes an area of mysterious emptiness, while the larger space of the mandala is filled with the progeny of the 'marriage' of soul and mind.

In such a mandala, the circumference ceases to have the character we attribute to Saturn, lord of personal boundaries and of precise and rationalistic formulations which bind while they define. At this level Saturn is to be seen in its mythological aspect as 'ruler of the Golden Age', the age of truth and innocence during which every human being is purely and solely what he or she is meant to be—the true exemplar of his or her dharma. The Saturnian mind is a crystal lens through which the universal focuses itself into the personal. When the open-center mandala is flooded with the light and power of the greater Whole, the boundaries of this smaller whole become translucent and, I might say, *transpowered*. Power passes through them and radiates beyond them, inspiring and blessing all the beings the illumined individual touches—and touching them ever so little transforms them.

This, however, can only gradually occur. It occurs when the four fundamental faculties displayed by the I-centered consciousness—sensation, feeling, thinking, intuition*—and the fifth principle emanating from the I-center, the will, have become repolarized and transmuted. This is at least one aspect of the alchemical Great Work—another aspect being the transsubstantiation of matter, once it is freed from the constraints and often the perversions brought to its basic substance and modes of operation by sociocultural and personal-individual factors.

On the transpersonal way, what is represented by the four angles of the birth-chart that has become an open-center mandala becomes subservient to the light that flows through the open core. This light is symbolically the light that circulates throughout the galaxy and is actually

---

*Cf. Chapter 4, p. 81.

the spiritual essence of the planetary Being whose multi-faceted and multilevel manifestation in the Earth's biosphere we speak of as mankind. But this galactic light—which a Christian mystic might think of and adore as the ineffable love of Christ—has also a focalizing center giving it a particular rhythm, tone, and intensity. This center is a particular star. It is the star at the zenith of the birthplace at the time of the first inhalation of air, because this zenith point is the symbol of the *link* between an individualized form of consciousness and the cosmic, all-embracing consciousness of the galactic Being.

In a sense, this link may be called the 'Higher Self.' It is rather SELF—the metacosmic principle of Unity, ONE—operating as and through a 'star.' It operates when this star succeeds in arousing the closed-center mandala of personality and its individualized and autistic I-center to the realization that its mandala-space constitutes but a single drop in the vast ocean of galactic space. This space, however, should be thought of as an 'ocean' of light. Within it the illumined individual can become a gem of translucent and sparkling beauty—and ancient esoteric traditions in Buddhist lands have spoken of the Diamond Soul.

The precisely structured and polished substance of this Diamond Soul is the product of the indissoluble union of the soul and the mind. It can be symbolized astrologically by a chart in which the fourfold pattern created by the cross of horizon and meridian is essentially replaced by an *hexagonal division*. This sixfold structure makes it possible for the light of the 'star' to radiate through the darkness of the biological level. The number 6 symbolizes the union of spirit and matter. In astrology, each of the six powers that are differentiated aspects of the galactic light that pours through the open center of the chart-mandala is considered a bipolar unit—masculine and feminine.* Thus the birth-chart has twelve houses, two successive houses constituting one unit. Seen at the lower levels, such a chart is only the biological *reflection* of the spiritual

---

*In my book, *An Astrological Mandala: The cycle of transformation and its 360 symbolic phases* (New York: Random House, 1973), Part III,

Form, the Diamond Soul. This spiritual Form becomes filled with light and love when what was at first only a body, then a person, and later on an individual, reaches the transindividual state. The human 'I' then becomes the agent of a star—the 'Son' of a divine Being.

Until such a culmination and completion of the trans-personal process is actually reached, the framework of the houses based upon the fourfold division defined by the cross of horizon and meridian—each of the four sectors being subdivided into three areas of experience—retains its fundamental meaning as the pattern of operation for karma at the human stage of evolution, at least once the mind—the essential human factor—begins to develop concretely and, in the course of time, independently of biological compulsions and cultural assumptions. But on the transpersonal path, karma is being transmuted into dharma; therefore the character of the twelve basic areas of human experience represented by the natal houses is gradually raised to a higher level, or rather to the level of what I will call *transobjectivity*.

Transobjectivity is not subjectivity. It refers to objective and concrete experiences which are no longer taken to be what they would appear to be to most people—i.e., as mere physical events—but are instead understood as symbols of archetypal phases of universal processes. In other words, transpersonal individuals live their lives-in-transformation

---

pages 304-311, I relate the six basic powers of the Diamond Soul— or in a cosmic sense, of the *Anima Mundi* (the World Soul)— to the six pairs (masculine and feminine) of zodiacal signs. One evidently can consider the twelve zodiacal signs as the Houses—or traditionally the 'mansions'—of the Sun. The solar system as a whole becomes a cosmic mandala, for at that level the astrologer should be able to understand that the Sun is not merely a mass of matter in the plasma state, but more truly a 'window' through which the power that whirls through galactic space constantly pours out upon the contents of the heliocosm. Occultists claim that we do not see the real Sun, but only what pours through it.

Such an approach, however, has (astrologically speaking) valid and workable meaning only in terms of a truly galactic kind of astrology; and we do not have as yet sufficient knowledge of *the whole* Milky Way to attribute a realistic significance to its component stars or groups of stars.

not in terms of *particular circumstances* given a strictly personal or perhaps aleatory interpretation, but in terms of *universal principles* and archetypal, non-personal meanings and purposes. They see *through* what others would call personal problems or interpersonal forces. Such a way of life is therefore quite radically different from what is advocated today in terms of purely 'personal growth' and the instant satisfaction of every desire, sexual and otherwise—just as it differs from the way of life of people who pass their lives determined by the assumptions and traditions of their society and culture.

The practice of transpersonal astrology is extremely difficult, because one has to see *through* what is considered the usual meaning of every factor being studied—and this includes both astrological factors in the client's birth-chart, transits and progressions, *and* existential factors in the client's life. One has to sense or intuitively perceive what is possible *through* what is. One has to sense the pull of the future in the hesitations that confuse the present state of consciousness. And if the astrologer is sure of the exact moment of the first breath of his or her client, if thus the exact zodiacal degree of the Ascendant of the birth-chart can be surely ascertained, the symbol of that degree* can be of profound significance as a clue to the character of the client's dharma, and therefore to the spirit in which he or she is able to proceed along the transpersonal way. But the interpretation of symbols is not easy; many extremely intelligent individuals bring to the task a socioculturally-molded mind; they allow themselves to be impressed by the external implications of a pictorial scene instead of trying to discover the deeper workings of basic principles *through* appearances. The transpersonal way is indeed always a way

---

*For a study of the Sabian Symbols for each degree of the zodiac, I refer the reader to my book *An Astrological Mandala: The cycle of transformations and its 360 symbolic phases* (New York: Random House, 1973).

*through* what it is. It is the evocation of the possible, even *through* the impossible.†

---

†In the spirit of the latter portion of this chapter, I also refer the reader to my book *An Astrological Triptych*, specifically Part II, "The Way Through" (New York: A.S.I. Publications, 1978).

# 8

# PROGRESSIONS AND TRANSITS

## Personality as an Unfolding Process

In dealing with any process of growth or basic transformation, one has not only to envision, at least along
broad and tentative lines, the possible end of the process,
one should also be able to discover *when* its successive
phases can be expected, and to learn about the conditions
under which the periods of transition from phase to phase
are likely to occur.

Two factors are implied in any change taking place in
an organism or organized system of social activity: (1) the
necessary *internal readjustment* of the organism and its
functions in order to meet successfully what is involved in
the change, whether this requires expansion, contraction,
or radical reorganization, and (2) the environment's
reaction to the change. The 'environment' may be the
family or society, and its reaction may be actual or
expected by the changing organism. Also, in many
instances, the internal change will be the result of external
causes, of important events taking place in the biosphere,
family, and/or society, in which one operates, making internal changes necessary.

If we consider a birth-chart the symbolic seed of an
individual personality, we can readily see that the growth
of the germinating seed into a large tree depends, on the
one hand, on the inner rhythm of the natural process of
unfoldment of seed-potentialities into the actualized form

of the tree, and on the other hand, upon weather conditions, sunshine and rain, and what insects, large animals, and human beings might do to the growing tree.

Astrology provides techniques for dealing with these two kinds of factors. The timing of inner changes in the process of biopsychic and mental-spiritual unfoldment of a particular person can be deduced from the study of what are broadly called *progressions*—of which there are several kinds. Another type of timing is derived from the actual motions of the planets—day after day, year after year—after the birth-moment: the *transits*.

These two types of techniques should be clearly differentiated, but, unfortunately, they are usually not. In one sense, *both* progressions and transits are the results of the fact that a birth-chart is a snapshot taken of a single moment in the continuous process of cosmic change, and that the planets whose positions are marked in the birth-chart keep moving; on the other hand, in progressions this motion is given a restricted and very special character, which is essentially different from what it has in transits. By mixing up the two techniques and not keeping the types of indications they provide strictly separate, astrologers lose the possibility of getting a clear view of the relationship between an individual's inner growth and the impact of the biopsychic and social environment upon this growth. Moreover, astrologers are taught *how to* calculate or observe progressions and transits, and *how to* interpret them according to keywords and formulas, but not *why* they should be considered valid.

In the techniques of progressions and transits, the new positions of the planets are usually referred to the birth-chart, which remains the foundation for astrological judgment—as it must be if we are concerned with the karma and dharma of an individual person. But astrologers also use a third approach in which the state of the solar system on any day and hour is studied with no reference to an individual's birth-chart—or in the case of the popular 'sun-sign-astrology', only to a person's natal sun-sign. The astrologer then assumes that the state of the solar system as a whole is reflected in that of the biosphere: "As above, so below." Thus, the tensions represented in the sky by a square of, say, Mars and Saturn can be expected to manifest in all living organisms within the biosphere as a tension between the impulsive, outgoing Mars-function and the limiting, contracting Saturn-function: in *all* living organisms in the biosphere and not merely in individual cases.

Granted that such an effect exists, it can be compared to that of the weather. Yet the weather is a factor affecting only a particular locality, while the state of the solar system—the sum-total of all the currents of energy generated by the motions of all material masses with the strong electromagnetic field of the solar system—should affect the whole Earth, or at least the areas of the globe under the direct line of impact, and everything in that area. The determination of what constitutes a 'direct line of impact' is a very controversial matter; and so is the often postulated correspondence between geographical areas (or nations) and zodiacal signs. These matters belong to the field of 'mundane astrology', however, and they cannot be covered in this book. I mention them here because they do not properly belong to the category of transits either, for this word refers to the passage of one moving body across another which is either practically non-moving or moving more slowly.

In the following I shall suggest what may be a more realistic explanation of why secondary (or solar) progressions are significant and what they specifically reveal; then I shall deal with transits. Both techniques can be used at all levels of interpretation, but I have so far refrained from mentioning them because their application at the first three levels has been formulated in detail in many books, but primarily in terms of a predictive type of astrology.

At the individual level of interpretation, transits and progressions have much the same meaning as the one I will now explain in relation to a transpersonal interpretation. But at the individual level, the birth-chart is the dominant factor, because a strictly individual life should lead, in principle, to the fulfillment of what was potential in the natal chart. In transpersonal astrology, on the other hand, the dominant concern of the astrologer is to understand the dynamism and rhythm of the transformative process itself. The birth-chart is only the starting point of this process, which even physical death may not end—if the individual has succeeded in raising his or her I-center to the transindividual (or symbolically, the 'galactic') level. From the transpersonal point of view, 'rebirth' may be more significant than 'birth', *if* the karma of the past has been lived through, absorbed and neutralized. But until this is accomplished—a rare occurrence—the natal foundation of the personality, with all it implies and all the future possibilities it may evoke, remains an essential base of operation.

## Secondary or 'Solar' Progressions

According to the principle of this type of progressions—today by the most commonly used—what occurs in the sky during the day following birth gives us symbolic information concerning what can be expected to happen during the first year of actual living. The positions of celestial bodies 48 hours after the birth-moment thus symbolize the biopsychic condition of the infant as he or she begins a third year of life. The astrologer finds out what the 'progressed' positions of all the planets will be when the client has passed his or her twenty-first birthday by looking for them in the ephemeris for the year of the client's birth, 21 days after the actual day of birth. The usually stated formula for such progressions is 'one day in the ephemeris equals one year of actual living.'

The value of such a symbolic procedure is constantly demonstrated, but the character and meaning of the information thus gained are often either exaggerated or wrongly interpreted. Most astrologers do not even question why it is that the technique gives significant results. They simply use the one-day-for-a-year formula as if there were nothing puzzling about it. Some astrologers with a more inquiring and philosophical type of mind have tried to find the logic in this correspondence, and the best explanation has been that *any whole cycle of motion can in some way be considered analogical to any other cycle.* Thus the day cycle produced by a complete rotation of the Earth on its axis is analogical to a year cycle produced by the Earth's revolution around the Sun—or, on a still larger scale, to one complete gyration of the polar axis in nearly 26,000 years (the cycle usually referred to as the cycle of 'precession of the equinoxes').*

In spatial terms this would also mean that the Earth's equator (any point on it accomplishing a complete rotation in one day) symbolically 'corresponds' to the Earth's orbit—that is, in astronomical terms, to the ecliptic, and astrologically speaking, to the (tropical) zodiac. This is one way in which the surface of the globe has often been divided into twelve longitudinal zones, each being made to correspond to (or be 'ruled' by) one sign of the zodiac.†

---

*Cf. my book, The Astrology of Personality (1936), especially Chapter 4, "A Key to Astrological Symbolism", and in terms of the historical significance of the cycle, Astrological Timing: The Transition to the New Age.

†A great deal of confusion has been spread by the use of the 'solar arc' method of calculating secondary progressions. In this technique all planets each day (or year) after birth are supposed to move forward at the same speed as the Sun does. This procedure actually refers to what Sepharial called the Radix System, which was meant as a simplification of the more involved 'primary directions' dealing with the daily cycle of the Earth's rotation. Everything in the birth-chart was moved ahead a whole degree for each year of actual living. Later on, the average rate of the Sun's motion (0° 59′ 08″) was substituted to the archetypal measure of one degree. This, I believe, is not a sound procedure, considering that these systems are purely symbolic. In an archetypal sense, the year has 360 days. From an existential point of view, the ratio between the lengths of any two cycles is never a whole number. The reason for this is that in the realm of actual existence, the immense multiplicity of interrelationships in operation constantly introduces a factor of indeterminacy. Nothing is ever exactly what it was meant to be. In principle, 360 rotations of the Earth should correspond exactly to a complete revolution around the Sun; but in fact an infinitely complex set of pressures slightly lessen the Earth's speed as it moves along its orbit.

In The Astrology of Personality, I gave a different interpretation to the Radix Directions, speaking of them as the translation of space-values (one zodiacal degree) into a time-value (one year of human time). This technique, when applied to the degree distances between important factors in the birth-chart, gives very basic results which mainly refer to the karmic structure of a human life. It can be profitably applied to the distances between planets and angles in rectification, when the exact birthtime is not known, but it must not be confused with secondary progressions.

Such a type of justification for the technique of secondary progressions is abstract and symbolic, and I had accepted it as valid until some years ago, when I realized that today one might consider the ideal, complete life-cycle of a human being to be about 90 years; and that in order for the prenatal period of gestation of a human being to cover a full yearly cycle of the Sun-to-Earth relationship, it would have to last some 90 more days. One might assume that since the Sun is the source of all life on Earth, in order for the life-force in a newborn baby to be fully developed, the *formative period of gestation* should have to encompass a whole yearly cycle.

The next question to come to mind is this: why should this *entire* formative period be passed in the *closed* field of a physical womb? And the answer is that while the physical body of a human being is normally developed in the mother's womb in nine months, the part of the total human being that is more than a physical body requires for its development 90 more days (3 months) in a relatively *open* field—a field in which the organism, by breathing air, is potentially related to all other living organisms in the biosphere (as air circulates around the globe quite rapidly)—organisms which also breathe air. In the field represented by the home, the baby comes in contact with people and experiences the basic rhythms of life. The baby's senses react to light, heat, moisture. He or she experiences hunger, pain, and we may assume, a sense of isolation in a strange world. Yet the baby is still held within a 'psychic womb'—primarily the mother's psyche, especially when he or she is breast-fed, and truly loved.

All these primordial and basic experiences and affects are necessary for the development of the psychic nature of the child, and for the development of what I mean by *intelligence*. I have defined psychism as the power that integrates a human being into his or her community and culture (and first of all his or her family environment). This power, binding as it is, is as necessary for the growth of a fully developed personality as the nine months in the physical womb are necessary for the formation of the physical body. By 'intelligence' I mean the capacity inherent in a human being to make whatever adjustments are needed to successfully operate in a biological, and, especially, a sociocultural environment. Biological adjustments are at first entirely instinctual and remain so at their deepest level when life-or-death situations suddenly arise; but a person's adjustments to society—to family, religion, school, peer group, and business—require a conscious and deliberate process of adaptation, which is really what is meant by 'intelligence'. In its more primitive form, intelligence is cunning. In school it is the ability to deal not only with the mass of knowledge one is supposed to remember and assimilate, but with what teachers and the whole educational system expect of a student. What we call 'intelligence tests' are given to ascertain the ability a person has to function effectively and in a normal way in a *particular* society and culture.

Recently publicized data indicating the crucial importance of the experiences to which a baby is subjected during the first weeks of his or her existence may be thought to provide a general, but existential and concrete, support to my interpretation of the reason why progressions can be exceedingly significant if used in the proper manner. This, however, does not alter the fact that progressions have a symbolic character. For example, it would be rather absurd literally to expect that bringing a baby to a doctor on the third or fifth day after its birth—or a visit by the grandparents on one of those days—would have definite repercussions on the course of events during the baby's third or fifth years of life. Yet in some instances, an apparently routine event might leave a deep psychic impression which could produce a psychosomatic reaction at a later date. Generally speaking, astrological progressions do not refer directly to concrete events; they symbolize the particular manner in which the more-than-physical, psychic and mental, parts of the human personality develop. Concrete events evidently affect this process of growth; but one might also reverse the situation and believe that it is the character of the process which, according to the newborn's karma, precipitates outer events of various types.

In the ninety days that follow birth, the Sun moves about 90 degrees, thus through three zodiacal signs (or possibly four, if one is born with the Sun at the very end of a sign). During that period only the planets closer to the

Sun than Jupiter advance far from their natal positions; some may even regress a few degrees after the day of birth. The more distant planets, from Jupiter outwards, move only very short distances, either forward or (during their retrograde periods) backward. The Moon alone completes not only one, but three turns of the zodiac—its sidereal period lasting 27⅓ days, equivalent in progressions to 27⅓ years.

The passage of the progressed Moon through each of the twelve houses of the birth-chart has therefore a unique meaning. As it passes through a house, the progressed Moon indicates the field of experience in which the development of the intelligence and the psychic nature of the person can be expected most significantly and/or successfully to operate. The first revolution of the progressed Moon is primarily a period of formation; the second, one of personal or individual expression and at least relative achievement—if all goes well. If the individual remains solely at the level of individual consciousness, the third period, after the 56th year, should be one of either personal fulfillment or gradual degeneration or crystallization. If, however, the individual has deliberately and consciously entered the path of radical transformation and remained on it, the last third of the life can be the most important, as it may bring clearer and steadier transpersonal realizations, and the ability to radiate at least a degree of mature and spiritually illumined wisdom.

The passage of the progressed Moon over each of the four Angles of the natal chart usually coincides with, and helps us interpret, some important inner or outer changes in a person's life and consciousness. The passage over the Ascendant is particularly important, for it often correlates with a change in one's environment or in one's psychological or physical relation to the environment. The change should lead to some kind of personal readjustment, perhaps the readjustment of one's intuitive feeling of identity in terms of the new environment or of a new realization of the meaning and value of the already familiar life-situation—the sense of individual selfhood being always intimately related to and most often conditioned by the various kinds of close relationships and associations one has entered, positive or negative as these may be.

When the progressed Moon crosses the Descendant of the birth-chart, changes in relationships are often expectable, or rather as this progression is about to occur one should try to pay closer attention to the quality of the relationships one is involved in, and to reassess their value.

The crossing of the natal Nadir (the cusp of the fourth house) by the progressed Moon may stir the feelings and should impel one to become more objective to what these feelings are and arise from—perhaps the home situation. As the progressed Moon crosses the Midheaven, a new approach to one's mental, social, or professional activities may seem valuable, if not imperative.

In my book *The Astrological Houses,** I discussed the basic meanings of the houses considered as categories or fields of experience, and I shall only briefly summarize here the characteristics which are of most value in terms of the progressed Moon's passage through them.

In the first house, a person tends to experience the results of being-an-individual; in the second, that of having to use and manage resources or possessions—and, more deeply still, the experience of 'potency' or lack of potency in any field. As the progressed Moon passes through the third house, a person would do well to focus his or her attention on problems dealing with the family environment, the neighborhood or matters concerning a learning situation—and as the progressed Moon crosses the I. C. into the fourth house, the focus should shift to defining one's personal space, whether in a physical or psychospiritual sense. This includes matters concerning one's place in one's home and/or country, and one's relation to the parent who most deeply affects the roots of one's feeling nature.

The fifth house refers to experiences resulting from desiring to be or seeing oneself multiplied in a biological or psychological progeny; the sixth house to the realization that it is necessary, willingly or not, to fit into

---

*(New York: Doubleday & Co., 1972)

some kind of sociocultural or interpersonal pattern of development—and often of 'service' at whatever level service may be asked of the person. The seventh house is the field of experiences produced by associating with, or merging one's identity into, the life of another or several partners for an implicit common purpose. In the eighth house, a person experiences the results of partnership in terms of set patterns of social or 'occult' activities; this is the house of business (the result of contractual agreements), and of communal rituals (whether sociocultural or religious), in which a number of people participate.

As the progressed Moon passes through the ninth house, a person would do well to focus on the opportunities to expand and to fit, more meaningfully or successfully, into either legalistic, intellectual-academic, or religious-cosmic patterns. This should lead to a more significant or valuable type of participation in one's community or nation—thus to professional or public experiences adding a larger dimension to one's field of activity; all of which relates to the tenth house. In the eleventh house, this tenth house type of participation will show its results—as various kinds of social and cultural enjoyments and entertainment, or as frustration and experiences of revolt or transformative activity. In the twelfth house, the results of an entire cycle of experience have to be concentrated upon, accounts should be closed, and a person should prepare to enter a new cycle, perhaps at a higher level of consciousness.

What has just been said refers more particularly to the personal and individual levels of interpretation, but these have to be considered when one deals with progressions because it is very rare for a young person before the age of 28 to definitely commit his or her being to the ideal of radical transformation. What may seem to be such a commitment refers most likely to the process of individualization and liberation from family and/or sociocultural patterns of behavior, feeling, and thinking. In the vast majority of cases, transpersonal realizations emerge out of the much-publicized crisis of the forties—which I once called adolescence in reverse. Yet under the pressure of the at least partial breakdown of our traditional Western culture and religion, and often through the action of psychedelic drugs, young people in their twenties experience at least a yearning for transcendent realities and a presentiment of what they entail. This, in many instances, leads to an intense, though not always steady and lasting, involvement in mystical or pseudomystical groups and practices, especially the practice of some kind of 'meditation'.

Every house of a chart can refer to several levels of experiences. A person-centered interpretation primarily stresses personal experiences to which a meaning is given in the light of the ideal of personality integration and fulfillment. On the other hand, a transpersonal type of interpretation would normally see, in the passage of the progressed Moon through a natal house, a special opportunity to deliberately adapt the experiences which the house symbolizes to the goal of transformation. The twelve houses can thus become twelve stations on the transpersonal way—the first house and the Ascendant which begins it marking, at least theoretically, the decision to consciously change one's sense of identity. As we already saw, on the transpersonal path the Moon can be interpreted as the 'soul'; thus, lunar progressions can sometimes be interpreted as referring to the relation of this soul—as I have defined the term in preceding chapters —to the 'higher collectivity' rather than merely to the process of constant adjustment to the 'lower collectivity' represented by family and society.

## Progressed Lunation Cycle: Progressed-to-Natal vs. Progressed-to-Progressed Considerations

While the progression of the Moon through the houses and in contact with natal planets in these houses are significant, because the Moon should always be intimately linked with the Sun, the most important cycle of progressions to be considered is what I have called 'the progressed lunation cycle.' The different periods in this soli-lunar cycle are made obvious by the ever-changing size of the Moon during the 30 days this cycle lasts. What changes, however, is not the Moon itself, but the relationship between the Sun and the Moon as seen from the Earth. The progressed lunation cycle therefore is the cycle of relationship between the progressed Moon and the progressed Sun.

The progressed lunation cycle no longer strictly belongs to the category of progressions in which a moving planet is referred to the natal position of other planets. In technical terms, the lunation cycle is a *progressed-to-progressed* cycle, whereas the above-mentioned progressions of the Moon through the houses, as it forms aspects to the planets of the birth-chart, refer to the *progressed-to-natal* category of relationships.

In *progressed-to-natal* progressions, the astrologer deals with the relationship between the seed-in-the-beginning (the birth-chart), and what has emerged from it at one or another moment in the process of unfoldment and self-actualization. This approach and technique is particularly valid in a strictly person-centered interpretation because, as I have said, at that level personal growth is essentially considered the actualization of a definite set of potentialities symbolically described in the birth-chart. Thus any new phase of growth should validly be referred to or compared with the original seed-potential. What occurs in the new phase of development may either help or endanger the hoped-for total and harmonious fulfillment of what was in the seed-in-the-beginning (and can be said to remain—perhaps within the genetic structure or perhaps in an electromagnetic 'design body', *linga sharira* in Sanskrit).

On the other hand, *progressed-to-progressed* indications increase in significance when an individual has become definitely intent on radical self-transformation, and therefore pays less and less attention to the past from which he or she is consciously emerging. From the transpersonal point of view, the progressed lunation cycle, as a progressed-to-progressed cycle, establishes the basic rhythm on whose dynamic foundation an individual's attempts at radical self-transformation operate. From such a transpersonal point of view, the progressed lunation cycle serves a purpose broadly similar, in terms of *process,* to that which the birth-chart has in terms of *individual structure of being.* Yet, in order to see how far one has moved away from what originally had been a determining and binding factor, one can refer the progressed lunation cycle to the natal chart.

I personally do so by marking on the outside of the natal chart the position of each progressed New Moon. The natal house in which the first progressed New Moon after birth occurs may not be the house in which the natal Sun is located. If it is not, a new house (and the life experiences to which it refers), at least temporarily receives the life-accent. The places of the succeeding New Moons inevitably fall in subsequent houses, as they occur about 30 and 60 degrees ahead of the position of the first New Moon. The zodiacal degrees on which they occur, and also of the progressed Sun and progressed Moon when in opposition (progressed Full Moons), are often most significant, the symbol of the degree (in the Sabian series) giving a clue to the overall character of the new phase of personality-unfoldment the progressed New Moon begins, at least until the progressed Full Moon some fifteen years later.*

Recently, however, Antony Milner, a graphic artist as well as astrologer, has designed charts especially for the study of all the phases of the progressed lunation cycle in itself—thus entirely as a progressed-to-progressed cycle of planetary relationship. A visual symbol of the whole process is provided which has been found to be extremely helpful in giving to students and clients a vividly experiential picture of the development of their life and

---

*For a study of the meaning of degree symbols in astrology, I refer the reader to my book *An Astrological Mandala: The cycle of transformations and its 360 symbolic phases* (New York: Random House, 1973). The extraordinary manner in which the Sabian Symbols were obtained, the remarkable inner structure of the entire series of the 360 symbols, their modern character and how they should be used, is explained at length in that book, written in 1972 but preceded, many years ago, by a series of articles on the subject (American Astrology, May, 1954 - October, 1957).

personality during a 30-year period.* While this development in most cases occurs at the level of the gradual process of individualization or of personal fulfillment in terms of a particular, cultural way of life, it can just as well be interpreted at the level of a transpersonal process. In such a case, the progressed Full Moon is particularly important, because it marks, at least potentially, the beginning of a psychomental process of discovery or recovery as the result of what had occurred during the fifteen years since the preceding progressed New Moon.

The first fifteen years of the progressed lunation cycle are usually related to the unfoldment of some new impulse or life-opportunity having been released around the progressed New Moon—it most often had been developing during the preceding two or three years in the inner life, or even in terms of outer events acting as a necessary prelude to the more definite start at the time of the progressed New Moon. The fifteen-year period following the progressed Full Moon theoretically operates in two ways: (1) The mechanisms of action that had been built or grew up during the waxing half of the cycle tend slowly (or sometimes suddenly around the time of the progressed Full Moon) to lose their efficacy or their power to forcefully draw the attention of the maturing I-consciousness; (2) at the same time, a process of mental development is given an opportunity to unfold its potentialities. What had mainly been physical and social or cultural activity (or the acquisition of a new technique or capability), during the waxing hemicycle of the progressed lunation cycle is, if not replaced by, at least combined with and inspired by, a deeper, more objective or transcendent development of the mind—a development having its origin around the time of the progressed Full Moon.

On the transpersonal path, a progressed Full Moon may coincide with some kind of 'illumination' or the intuitive

---

*Lunation cycle phase mandalas designed by Antony Milner for this purpose are available for purchase from Rudhyar Books and Tapes, 3635 Lupine Avenue, Palo Alto, CA 94303. For a detailed explanation of how to use the progressed lunation cycle, see my book, *The Lunation Cycle* (Boulder, Colo.; Shambhala Publications, 1971), and *The Lunation Process in Astrological Guidance* by Leyla Rael (New York, A.S.I., 1979).

revelation of a new goal and purpose. It can be an excellent time for withdrawing from and beginning to transcend the past, especially if what had occurred since the progressed New Moon has proven frustrating or illusory. It usually is a moment of choice—thus a 'crisis'— even though at first the choice is not yet clearly definable. It becomes clearer at the progressed Last Quarter when a final confrontation with what remains of the past often occurs. About three years before the coming progressed New Moon, the transition between the closing progressed lunation cycle and the next one begins. This is what I have called the 'Balsamic' (an old alchemical term) or 'seed' period of the 30-year cycle. It is often a life-phase during which transformative forces are best able to operate. If one realizes that such a period has begun, one should feel particularly open—yet discriminating—to any opportunity for changes that may come one's way.

At any level of astrological practice, the progressed lunation cycle can be an extremely valuable psychological tool. The lives of individuals groping for a basic under-standing of why and exactly how they had to pass through a series of perhaps traumatic experiences have been illumined and at least partially transformed by its use. Transformation cannot be truly effective unless the individual has become objective to the events of the past and—the next step—detached from them. One, however, is never entirely detached from a past one still does not understand, and with which one has not come to terms and accepted as a necessary step in the process of developing character and consciousness. The sense of guilt—or even of personal inferiority—is born of lack of objectivity and understanding. On the transpersonal path, guilt and inferiority complexes are largely responsible for either some kind of collapse based on a subtle type of defeatism and mistrust of one's power, or—by compensa-tion—for the kind of price that is bound to insecurity and fear.

In order to overcome these repressed, unconscious, or semi-conscious feelings, the progressed lunation cycle and all that relates to it can be an excellent tool. If well used by an *astro-psychologist*, it can be more effective and safer than 'regressions' in semi-hypnotic states, and even than dream-analysis—which, when made by the dreamer may be too subjective, and when made by most psychologists, too dependent upon intellectual concepts and specialized forms of training. Unfortunately, however, the progressed lunation cycle is still not used by most astrologers, perhaps because they seem unable to think in terms of whole processes—especially processes spanning several years—and because their training has prepared them to think primarily in terms of separate and isolated events.

An event has been defined in physics as the intersection of world-lines. But these world-lines are in fact curved; they are the abstraction of cyclic processes. To understand an event is to be able to perceive it not as an isolated entity, but as the intersection or conjunction of cosmic or planetary cycles. The event has to be perceived not by an 'I' involved in its own existence, prestige, or happiness, but by a mind able to embrace entire processes and to give meaning to all their phases. Theologians and philosophers have spoken of understanding an event *sub specie eternitatis*—but 'eternity' is a misunderstood and glamorized word which simply refers to the cyclic character of all existence. The Latin phrase simply means that existence can only be understood as a vast complex of cyclic processes. No event can be understood in isolation. It has not only a past and a future, but it is a combination of a vast number of cyclic activities at many levels.

Thus I repeat: progressions should *not* be interpreted in terms of precise, expectable occurrences. Astrology should not be a 'predictive science', or even merely a descriptive process in which all the described features remain basically isolated, because unrelated to a holistic grasp of the whole life-span, from birth-to-death. Especially at the transpersonal level, the realization of the direction or orientation of the entire life-process is an essential factor. Life has to be purposeful and meaningful—however distant the fulfillment of the purpose may seem. One should not attempt to define such a purpose in precise, concrete terms. Metaphysically speaking, there is no conceivable end to the process of transformation, because there is no end to the hierarchical series of wholes.

The spiritual life simply consists in *taking the next step* toward an open-ended future.

Another point should be made concerning the technique of progressions and the difference between progressed-to-natal and progressed-to-progressed aspects. In the first case, when the progressed Sun or Moon or any other planet reaches the place of a natal planet, the latter does not directly affect the progressing planet. A progressed Sun, for example, would bring to a natal Saturn power and light; but Saturn would not 'do' anything to the Sun. What might be said to happen is that at the age corresponding to the progressed-to-natal aspect, the life-force (the Sun) will tend to and should focus its attention upon all that Saturn represents in the circumstances defined by the birth-chart and manifest in the life. This, however, could have two kinds of results: on the one hand, the Saturnian sense of form, organization, and responsibility could be thrown into a sharper and clearer relief and probably aroused to action. On the other hand, however, whatever basic fears and sense of guilt or inferiority that exist in the psyche may be revealed. The Sun pours its light upon everything: a diamond will sparkle magnificently, a decaying fish will decay more quickly.

The situation is different in a progressed-to-progressed situation, because in such an aspect both planets are moving and, let us say, their conjunction is an actual fact in the sky a few days or weeks after the child was born. In this case, what is represented by the two planets can at that time be said to have blended in the psyche of the baby, and to have become the unconscious source of life developments which at a later age will potentially allow the individual to objectify and release whatever in infancy had been stored in the psychic depths.

According to the transpersonal approach to astrology, the progressed-to-natal aspects seem to mark particular times at which an opportunity to neutralize the *karma* of the past appears. The progressed-to-progressed aspects refer more characteristically to openings in life which allow the energy of *dharma* to operate through what is symbolized by the relationships between the planets forming the aspects. The progressed lunation cycle is of course a progressed-to-progressed cycle, and much can be gained from its study that may enable the intuitive astrologer to gauge objectively where the client stands—and to advise him or her concerning the kind of efforts and activities most conducive to foster a radical change in attitude and outlook.

## The Transits of the Planets

While progressions refer primarily to the development of tendencies of all kinds inherited from the past—genetic, cultural, spiritual—and all these internal tendencies operate mainly through the lunar and soli-lunar cycles, the interrelating cycles of the *transiting* planets should be interpreted specifically as patterns related to pressures and impacts coming from the outside. By the term 'outside' I mean here what is outside of the field of consciousness—outside of the realm over which the ego rules, and whose center is 'I', the song of individual selfhood, often turning into a harsh series of discords. The 'outside' is the collectivity in relation to the individual. But, as we have already seen, there are several kinds of collectivities. At each level at which a human being operates, his or her activities are influenced by and often have to fit into rigid collective patterns, not only of behavior, but—though the person may not be fully aware of this—of feeling-responses and thought.

At the biological level, 'collectivity' refers to the whole biosphere, and to human nature's reactions to changes, whether they be regular seasonal changes or cataclysms. At the next higher level, collectivity has a sociocultural character; transits refer to the way a nation and its various institutions—political, religious, and commercial—impress their collective power upon the men, women, and children whose lives they control, not only outwardly, but psychically. Transits then act primarily upon the psychism that binds people, and as societies become more complex and more mentally structured and active, what was at first only 'psychic' takes increasingly more intellectual or mental forms. The psychomental pressures, symbolized by the transits, in turn produce—directly or indirectly—concrete and physical-material results, what we call 'events.'

When at a certain stage of the process of individualization, the consciousness of a person becomes evolved enough to become aware of the possibility—or the actual existence of—a contact with a realm of transindividual beings, this person can become directly and individually related to some aspect of the 'higher' collectivity which encompasses the spiritual aspect of mankind. A one-to-one relationship can be established between the human individual and the 'star' that symbolizes his or her transindividual selfhood, or a particular aspect of the 'galactic' consciousness operative in this higher collectivity may focus itself upon the mind of the individual on the transpersonal way. Before such a direct and individualized relationship is established, the higher collectivity can undoubtedly affect human beings, but the connection operates in a psychic and unconscious or semi-conscious manner, rather than as a direct and individualized line of influence.

Some scientifically-oriented astrologers who dismiss progressions as being 'symbolic' and not referring to actual facts are willing to accept transits as factual because they deal with what is actually happening day-by-day in the sky. But while a transiting planet is concretely observable, to speak of it in the astrological sense implies that one thinks of the natal positions of the planets as having been somehow indelibly stamped upon the human being, or of the shape of the universe surrounding a newborn as a kind of permanent enveloping structure. In this structure the natal planets would be like windows through which the 'rays' of transiting planets could pass. When Mars passes over the natal Venus-window a 'transit aspect' occurs; and theoretically the Mars energy affects and somewhat blends with whatever the Venus-type of activity and consciousness represent in the birth-chart and in the life of the person to whose birth-chart Mars' transit is being referred.

Another explanation is that at birth the organism of the baby is, in a sense, programmed to respond in an individual manner to the ever-changing interaction of ten variables—the planets (including the Sun and Moon). A simple illustration would be found in an ordinary alarm clock: when the moving hand of the clock passes over the alarm indicator set for a selected time of day, a bell rings. Whoever selected the time and set the clock jumps out of bed—or sometimes yawns and falls back to sleep. Each natal planet, the Angles of the chart, and other secondary factors could, according to this illustration, be considered indicators set once and for all at birth. When the day-by-day moving planets in the sky pass over (transit), the positions of these indicators around the face of the clock, the person can be expected to react. The character of the reaction depends on the nature of the planets involved, that is, of *both* the natal planet and the transiting planet.

These illustrations, however, leave unanswered the basic question posed by such explanations, which try so hard to appear concrete and factual. The only satisfactory way to approach the problem, at least in the present state of our knowledge, is to think of *both* the birth-chart and the transits as potent symbols. The birth-chart is the foundation of a person's life, from birth to death; the transiting planets represent the manner in which the solar system—or any 'greater whole' within which the little whole (the human being) operates—affects this foundation and the development of the lesser whole, the human being. It really does not matter how one tries to explain the way that occurs within a greater whole affects the lesser wholes it contains. One may speak of 'correspondence', 'synchronicity', or an 'inner clock' set at birth and continuing to run at its own speed while the solar system maintains its complex rhythmic patterns of ever-changing interplanetary relationships. All explanations are symbolic. The important point is to understand what each component of the symbolic system one uses refers to at the level at which one's attention is being focused.

In every situation with a cyclic character—that is, one that has a definite beginning, a growth process and an eventual ending—two factors are always present, because such an existential cycle starts with one single dynamic impulse which establishes a basically invariant rhythm of being, the 'unity aspect' (or *alpha*) of the cycle. We may call this unitarian impulse, and the form it takes, 'the Word' that is 'in the beginning', or the genetic code, or the archetype of the life-cycle, or the 'Tone' that sustains and keeps all the operations of a living organism integrated according to a relatively unique plan of existence. But whatever it is called, it is a permanent factor, at least within the scope of terrestrial existence.

When operating at a strictly biological level, a human being is not aware of the existence of such a primordial and invariant factor. It is spoken of in Genesis 2:7 as the 'living soul' breathed into the human form by the ruler of the realm of 'life' (the biosphere), the Biblical 'Lord God', Yod-He-Vau-He, the Tetragrammaton. The birth-chart of a single human being is a symbolic representation of this permanent factor, and the transits refer to the effects that conditions in the biosphere and the strictly physical environment have on the daily development of the biological functions and their psychic overtones.

At the level of a conscious human being operating in society, the birth-chart is to be considered the archetypal pattern of his or her personality—or we might say 'personhood.' When the person who has developed under the powerful influence of a particular language, religion, culture, and social way of life succeeds in asserting his or her own individual center, 'I', the birth-chart becomes a mandala symbol in which everything is referred to this autonomous center, its consciousness and its theoretically independent will-power.

At these two levels (sociocultural and individual), planetary transits refer to what the constantly changing conditions prevailing in the family, social, or business environment can do to the personality and individuality of a human being operating in that environment, as well as to his or her physical body and its functions.

As the individual begins to walk on the transpersonal path, the relation of the individual to his or her collectivity takes on another character. Then, planetary transits may often refer to situations that seem to disturb the process of transformation—as distractions, temptations, or challenges to the sincerity and dedicated will of the traveler on the path. The cultural enjoyments or achievements (for example, wealth or fame) which society may offer can be deterrents or tests indicated by planetary transits. But at this stage some of the transits may also be interpreted as—and they may actually be—attempts from this 'higher collectivity' of spiritual beings (the Pleroma) to intervene in the process of transpersonal overcoming of and detachment from culture and social concerns—and also from biological attachments of various kinds. Such 'interventions' are especially related to the transits of Uranus, Neptune, and Pluto, for these planets outside of the Saturnian boundaries of the solar system proper can be symbolically regarded as 'agents' or ambassadors of the galaxy whose function is to convey messages from the transindividual realm to the I-center of the mandala of personality, and also to serve as guideposts helping to orient the individual on his or her way to the 'star.'

The study of transits can be a fascinating exercise in intuition, if it is not more or less unconsciously conditioned by the textbook interpretation of what is supposed to happen when transiting planet A crosses over, opposes, or squares (or even forms a trine or sextile to), the natal position of planet B. In the case of the faster planets—Mercury, Venus, and Mars—with short periods of revolution around the zodiac, the entire repeated cycles of these planets should be studied in relation to a person's life and natal chart. Repetitive patterns may emerge from such a study, and recurrent events or internal feelings would point to factors in the personality that especially need to be understood and dismissed as irrelevant when one is engaged in the process of radical transformation. These factors may be strengthened by interpersonal contacts or made a repeated source of confusion and doubts by environmental pressures—for example, the pressures of one's peer group, or repeated bouts with a chronic illness.

Mercury and Venus transiting over natal planets may be related respectively to the passing influence, direct or indirect and insidious, that the cerebro-mental and emotional trends operating in a culture and its fashions have upon the people living in that society. And intellectual fashions are as much in evidence as fashions in clothing and group-behavior or interpersonal relationships such as marriage and love-affairs. We may believe that the way we feel and express ourselves emotionally is strictly our own, indeed, an absolutely personal matter; but this is a fantastic illusion, especially in our modern world where the media spread fast-changing fashions in every field of personal activity, feeling and thinking—witness the results of the movement of youth protest and the 'flower children' of the late Sixties.

In principle, Venus and Mars are intimately connected with personal emotions, and these too are far more determined by collective trends and pressures than we care to admit. What psychologists and educators like to call 'spontaneity' is, in the great majority of cases, the working out of unconsciously determining images, or of interpersonal influences assimilated by the psyche, but whose source has been forgotten.

The transits of Jupiter and Saturn are more specifically related to the larger aspects of collective living—to religion, the authorities, and the law. Jupiter takes about twelve years to circle the zodiac, and its passage through the natal houses at times shows the impact which money, wealth, expanded social contacts, or the desire to meet and work with people have on various fields of experience. Jupiter refers to expansion in general, but the possibility of expanding very often depends on the general conditions of business, of taxes, or of the way one's peer group reacts to religion, politics, or commerce. If Jupiter moves over a person's natal Sun or Ascendant, this does not need to mean that greater wealth or prestige is experienced, but rather that the Jupiterian factors in society will have a more focalized influence in the person's life during the time of the transit.

The nearly 30-year long cycle of Saturn is particularly important because it may interweave and react upon the also 30-year long progressed lunation cycle. The phases of these cycles do not operate simultaneously unless a person is born just at New Moon. While the progressed lunation cycles deal with the autonomous internal unfoldment of the birth-potential of the human being, the Saturn cycle refers primarily to the development of his or her sense of security and ego. During the first 30 years of life, a person largely depends upon his or her physical-emotional vitality—and in many cases also upon parental support—to give him or her a sense of security. In normal times, this sense of security takes, at the mental and emotional levels, the form of either total reliance upon a tradition and parental way of life, or of a revolt against the family and class environment—this revolt providing the youth with a negative kind of sustainment. Both alternatives, in fact, are usually experienced simultaneously, at least after puberty.

During the second 30-year cycle, the Saturnian sense of security takes, at least theoretically, an individualized character which was actually lacking before the first 'Saturn return'. The youth in his or her twenties, however, often pretends he or she is already truly an 'individual' completely self-motivated and secure in his or her identity. Yet he or she is still constantly affected by social and financial pressures which force the would-be-individual to respond to collective pressures in order to securely maintain this identity. After 30 the problems this poses should be handled more consciously and in terms of an inner sense of security. After the age of 60, the more or less 'retired' person may have found outer security in his investments, in the support of his or her children, or 'social security'—or in some cases in public prestige and fame. Even if these social props are missing, an individual may develop a deep and unshakeable sense of security on the basis of a philosophical or (more often) religious kind of understanding and acceptance of his or her destiny. This is the wisdom of old age. But if the experiences of the preceding Saturn cycles have been frustrating and embittering, and life has seemed dreadfully empty, Saturn's transits may bring rigidity and sclerosis to the organic and intellectual functions represented by the planets being transited.

Yet in most cases, when Saturn transits over the zodiacal degree occupied by a natal planet, one should not be led to expect some deeply sobering or at least dreary experiences, but rather the probability of some situation impelling the ego to deal more effectively with that life-function or aspect of the personality which the natal planet symbolizes. When Saturn passes over the natal

Sun, the vital forces may be negatively affected, and their tone lowered, but the cause of this should be found in either a previous weakening of the ego's stability, or in the impact of social-political or religious and ethical forces. These forces may operate from the 'outside', as for example a business failure caused by a national depression or change in fashion, or an encounter with the police which either was or was not justified. There are many instances of a person assuming a heavy business responsibility or an important and demanding political office when Saturn crossed his or her natal Sun. Saturnian forces may also operate 'within' the mind and psyche in terms of what used to be called 'one's conscience'—the product of a collective tradition which one may have refused to follow, yet which has remained entrenched in the subconscious (the collective psychism).

Transits of Uranus are likely either to cause sudden changes or to bring transformative processes to a focus in the area of the personality these transits affect. The 84-year Uranus cycle is extremely important in our present individualistic and intellectually-oriented society. I believe that, once a human being reaches an individualized status through the use of an effective and relatively independent mind, this 84-year span is the archetypal measure of life. This of course does not mean that a person cannot live longer; but if he or she does, forces beyond his or her individuality may be operating—some of which, however, may derive from a special genetic background, in turn related to particular biospheric conditions. The 90-year period produced by three 30-year long Saturn cycles may have much to do with living a few years beyond the 84 years of the Uranus cycle. As to the transit cycles of Neptune and Pluto—respectively 163.74 and 245.33 years—they transcend the field of a normal lifespan at this present time of human evolution. Their transiting squares and semisquares to their natal places as well as the full range of aspects they can make to other natal planets may symbolize disturbing or cathartic, but also potentially regenerative, crises of growth or identity.

The transits of these trans-Saturnian planets gain a particular importance as an individual walks on the transpersonal Path, because this individual has taken a step which, if he or she is sincere and persistent, brings him or her to the attention of the 'higher collectivity' of trans-individual beings. Especially when Uranus, Neptune, and Pluto pass over the Sun, the Moon, and the four Angles of the birth-chart, they often refer to definitely critical turning points in the life of such an individual, and the astrologer using a transpersonal approach has to be very careful in suggesting what meaning these crises might have in the process of repolarization of the mind and the activities of his or her client.

It is never possible, from strictly astrological data *only*, to predict what concrete forms such crises may take, and the transpersonal astrologer should certainly not indulge in definite predictions. At this transpersonal level, what *exactly* will happen is of no real interest. The essential requirement is to be truly open to the possibility of a radical transformation of any element within one's personality. The character of the I-center of this personality may be particularly affected when Uranus crosses, opposes, or squares the Sun. The conjunction of transiting Uranus with natal Sun almost infallibly correlates with a basic change in the life of an individual on the transpersonal path, often with what is called an identity-crisis. Yet the inertia of the Saturnian insistence on inner or outer security may not allow the crisis to release its deeper potential of transformation or reorientation.

If, for example, a person loses his or her job or public position when, let us say, Mars and Uranus pass over his or her natal Midheaven, such a person may experience discouragement or bitterness (especially if Pluto is also involved), and fight to be transferred to a similar job or use his or her knowledge of the job-market for the same purpose. The planetary transits can be considered indicators of an upsetting event, which an astrologer might have expected. But the individual who has his or her mind oriented toward a process of transformation would consider this loss of job under such aspects as life's 'revelation' that it was time for him or her to use this opportunity to transform whatever the Midheaven symbolizes *for him or her as an individual center of consciousness*—as an opportunity far deeper than merely passing from one job-situation to a similar one.

The astrologer's task at this transpersonal level is to evoke whatever seem to be new possibilities—whether of action or of understanding—to help the client 'relax the cramp in the conscious' of which Carl Jung spoke, yet without losing the faculty of discrimination.

A transit of Neptune may excite and confuse the part of the personality it contacts with glamorous visions or hopes inconsistent with the individual dharma. These often use the material with which the individual's religious tradition—or some other 'esoteric' teaching—had filled his or her mind. If this happens, a time often comes when Pluto will de-glamorize that mind and leave it empty and bewildered.

It is important to be aware of the rather extraordinary fact that the archetypal length of the cycles of these three transformative agents of the galaxy as they revolve around the Sun are so interrelated that two Uranus cycles equal one Neptune cycle, and three Neptune cycles, one Pluto cycle.* In other words, the operations of these three planets should be studied and understood as constituting a threefold process. What begins with Uranus, proceeds through Neptune and—as far as we are able to comprehend at this time—ends with Pluto. This does not mean that there is no planet beyond Pluto; one may have been discovered, but it may not be a planet in the same sense as the others. Even if it is, Pluto may still represent the end of a particular process—the total atomization of what was once a 'solid' structure. This process, symbolized by Uranus, Neptune, and Pluto, if successful should be followed by another phase referring to re-organization at a new level. I have symbolized this reorganization process under the name Proserpine—but Proserpine may not be a *visible* planet. It might remain invisible *if* the collective, planet-wide crisis of transformation now being experienced by mankind is not given a

---

*I have discussed the interactions between these cycles and the meaning of the passages of these three planets through each zodiacal sign in my book *The Sun is Also a Star* already-mentioned. The transits through the natal houses were treated in *The Astrological Houses*.

constructive meaning and ends in some kind of catastrophe.

Considered from a holistic point of view, the value of transits is that they help us divide a human life-span in several ways, and thus enable the astrologer to watch the unfolding of a complex pattern which can mean not only personal growth, but also transpersonal transformation. Seen from a *person-centered* point of view, this pattern is itself encompassed by the repetitive circle of birth, death, and new birth; what had been potential 'in seed' develops, reaches a degree of fulfillment, then disintegrates— leaving some kind of harvest and a definite amount of unspent energy and unfinished business, both of which in turn will condition a new life-cycle. This cyclic sequence constitutes what the Hindus called *samsara*—the wheel of birthing and dying—the wheel of karma, always revolving, producing new and often repetitive lives, all related to one another according to a 'horizontal' kind of relationship-in-time.

The *transpersonal* approach, especially when founded upon the principle of holarchy, evokes for us the possibility of another kind of process—a multilevel process that does not close upon itself. Such an approach postulates the interaction and interdependence of lesser and greater Wholes. It reveals the relative value and purpose of the 'I-realization' to which our Western world's individualism (or philosophical 'Personalism,' or occult monadology) has given an absolute character. It attempts to evoke through symbols of universalistic inter-action and interdependence the twofold interrelationships between levels of wholeness—the 'descent' of the higher being synchronous with the 'ascent' of the lower— and of their eventual meeting.

What results from this meeting—this 'marriage of Heaven and Earth'—is still, for most of us, a great mystery. Today it no longer needs to be a mystery; or rather, it can be understood and experienced as a 'Mystery' in the ancient sense of the word: a ritual celebration within which action instantly reveals its meaning, and consciousness and activity fuse into a poem of existence. At this stage of the development of con-sciousness, human existence can be considered and indeed experienced as a wholeness of being gradually realized through cyclic and multilevel processes of change. Each level has its place and function. Each level answers to a basic kind of need; and all needs and all solutions interact and interpenetrate.

In the same sense, all approaches to astrology, whether in the mode of analytical knowledge or of synthesizing wisdom, can be said to interact and interpenetrate. Every approach, if sincerely, honestly, and effectively followed, can meet the need of some kind of human being. Yet because mankind today has reached new levels of knowledge and should also attain higher levels of understanding, the need for new symbols and new levels of interpretation is a fact that can no longer be dismissed or circumvented. The transpersonal approach to astrology presents us with a way of thinking which can help us to bring into a more ordered and meaningful pattern the increasingly more complex experiences whose impacts may easily confuse or even bewilder our mind and feelings. Objectively and unemotionally watching the unfoldment of this pattern can bring periodic revelations to individuals intent on using whatever confronts them in the fullest and most transformative way possible.

# EPILOGUE

In concluding this book, a few essential points should once more be stressed.

The first is that while all astrologers, past and present, use the periodic motions of discs and points of light across the sky as symbolic means to discover the principles operative in a universe which they feel certain is ordered and meaningful, each cultural or religious tradition to which these astrologers belong interprets the order and meaning of the universe in a different manner. In other words, there is only one astrological field of observation—the sky and the motion of celestial lights across it—but many astrological systems and traditions. Similarly, one could say that all human beings have a religion which gives a particular form to their deep feeling of what the relation of Man to the universe as a whole is; but there are many religions, including those that deny the existence of what others call gods or God. One can also speak of science as the result of man's attempt to organize the knowledge he is able to obtain in one way or another; but each culture has its own characteristic manner of organizing and defining knowledge.

Each culture has thus a more or less characteristic religion, social organization, art, science, and astrology; and these equally important products of human consciousness can operate at one level or another, each level being defined by the character, quality, and inconclusiveness of the operative consciousness.

Astrology—just as religion, philosophy, the arts, or science—is a symbolic system. It interprets as well as organizes the results of collective—and in some special cases, individual—experience. To cast an astrological chart in the way it is done today is just as symbolical a process as painting an oil painting destined to be framed and exhibited in a home or museum, or writing a complex orchestral score, or filling a page of paper with algebraic formulas whose meaning only a trained mathematician can understand. All these totally different activities have essentially the same basic purpose: the formulation in a particular way of what human existence implies and means, whether the meaning given is personal or impersonal, positive or negative, harmonious or discordant.

Archaic astrologers spoke of the planets and stars as the light-bodies of gods; classical astrologers gave them mythological names symbolizing their assumed character; and modern astronomers see them as masses of matter in one state or another. These are different interpretations, using different symbols. Each was or is valid at the level of consciousness at which it was formulated. The names of the gods were mantrams, formulas of power—effective at the level at which the namers' consciousness operated and in the conditions of existence in which these namers lived and acted. In our technological era, the astronomers' and cosmophysicists' mathematical formulations are effective in enabling human beings to walk on the Moon or send radio messages via artificial satellites. Our modern technological universe is assuredly far vaster in a quantitative sense than the one of the old Chaldeans, but this does not necessarily imply that it is basically more significant or an inspiration for a more constructive, harmonious, and happy way of life.

In my approach to life, I assume that one can speak of a dynamic process of evolution from level to level; but other philosophers consider time and change as an illusion and assume that every possibility of existence is 'now', either actually spread through infinite space or contained within an 'absolute' state of being, beyond time and space. These are all interpretations of data finding their way by one path or another to the human consciousness—interpretations given a form by the mind using symbols. Whether these symbols are words, sounds, hieroglyphs, or numbers and algebraic formulas makes no essential difference. But the *practical* differences are enormous. If we fail to recognize them, we wind up in a state of not only mental, but also emotional confusion—for our emotions are conditioned and often predetermined by the symbolic picture we, individually and/or collectively, make of the universe and our place and function (or lack of function) in this picture.

We do not *know* what place we actually occupy in the universe, only the place we have in *our picture* of the universe. In some pictures we are at the center of the scene and everything revolves around us, including the attention of the God we vaguely describe as the transcendent Creator of the universe. In another picture we are slightly more evolved animals on a planet revolving with others around small star, the Sun, which is only a small unit far from the center of a galaxy whirling through space in which billions of other immensely distant galaxies are also whirling.

These are all pictures symbolically representing collective states of consciousness. Similarly, all the data used in astrology are symbols. The manner in which we use them and our purpose in using them determine our state of consciousness and the character or quality of our activity. As however, the practice of astrology most often implies the relation between a consultant and a client, it is highly important for the consultant to adapt his or her interpretation to the level at which the client is able or desirous to respond to this interpretation. If this is not done, the client either does not understand and is disappointed by what he or she is told, or else gives to the interpretation a meaning that could be psychologically destructive—or considers the whole experience below the level of his or her intelligence or expectations.

It is therefore most important for anyone—astrologer or client—to understand that, even within the field of an astrological consultation in which personal problems, traumatic memories, and eager expectations are discussed, there is not only one way of approaching these matters and the most relevant astrological data. Even if the astrologer is not expected to act as a fortune-teller but is instead known to use a mainly psychological approach, it is possible that the client's problems, and his or her own state of consciousness and life-purpose, belong to a level at which the astrologer is not able to effectively and empathetically operate. The potential client should therefore be aware that there are several levels at which birth-chart, progressions, and transits can be interpreted. If the client is not aware of this, the astrologer should nevertheless realize that the case he is asked to deal with may be beyond this full understanding.

Just as a general practitioner or family doctor confronted with a difficult pathological situation sends his patient to a specialist, so if an astrologer is only used to dealing with people whose problems fall in conventional categories and is unable to operate beyond the strictly personal level, he or she should send an individual whose consciousness and motives have a more transcendent character to an astrologer operating at a more individualized and perhaps transpersonal level. It would be senseless and potentially dangerous for a mystically inclined individual experiencing a period of doubt and temporary confusion—a 'dark night of the soul'—to go to a Freudian analyst for reassurance and guidance. At least such an individual should seek a Jungian psychologist.

The same situation can occur, and does occur today in many cases, with regard to the selection of an astrological consultant; and the problem this poses would presumably not be satisfactorily met by legalizing astrology and giving official diplomas to astrologers after a standardized kind of examination and test. Astrologers, as well as their critics, need to realize that there is not just one kind of astrology and only one level of interpetation. The level of interpretation should fit the level at which the person asking advice and guidance operates, or at least shows the possibility of effectively and relatively safely operating.

Unfortunately, in our society which in theory worships the ideal of individual freedom and individual equality, yet in fact functions in most instances according to collective values and standardized goals, it is difficult for most people—including psychologists, medical doctors, and astrologers—to accept the concept of a hierarchy of levels. Everybody has to be treated the same way, regardless of racial, cultural, class, and personal differences. Yet, wonderful and ideal though this concept of equality is *at a spiritual level,* it cannot constructively apply at the level of personal psychology and in terms of the most effective and meaningful way of meeting the problems of individuals. Any sensitive psychologist or astrologer is aware of this during a consultation, but in most cases there is a tendency for a consultant to seek safety in standardized techniques.

Impersonality and objectivity and a traditional or official interpretation of symptoms are needed up to a certain point; but they can also be means to evade responsibility and play safe. Astrological aphorisms or statistical percentages can indeed be devices making it easier for consultants neither too brilliant nor intuitive to avoid taking personal risks when faced with non-routine situations. Any subjective evaluation is avoided as being unscientific, but what is really meant is *unsafe.* Yet spirit is the subjective polarity of being. Religion refers to objective forms and collective symbols and values; spirituality essentially is a subjective factor.

What occurs during the process of radical transformation is that the subjective pole in an individualized field of human existence gradually shifts from one level to the next. The pleroma state of consciousness is a transindividual kind of subjectivity. The whole is subjectively present and conscious in every one of the billions of participants in its activity. One might speak here of *transsubjectivity,* though such a word has no realistic meaning except for those who have at least a faint glimpse of the implications of the transindividual state of being. The consciousness of the whole is present in all its parts, whose coherent and integrated activities bring to objective manifestation its subjectivity. At the pleroma level of transindividual existence, the whole does not have an I-center; because *the center is everywhere.* This is what the famous phrase of the French philosopher Pascal (who was probably not its first author) tries to convey by defining God as a circle whose center is everywhere and circumference nowhere.

According to the philosophy of holarchy I have been

presenting, the universe is not only a hierarchy of wholes; each level of wholeness, abstractly speaking, is characterized by a *quantitatively* immensely larger circumference; and each change of level of wholeness requires a new *qualitative* relationship between center and circumference—thus between subjectivity and objectivity. This, of course, is a highly metaphysical concept, but it also has extremely practical implications. The evolutionary path that individualized human beings can and eventually will tread does not lead to bigger and better men and women, but to 'more-than-man'.*

Transpersonal astrology likewise is not to be thought of as a bigger and better kind of astrology; it is 'more-than-astrology'. It does not deal with a 'whole-ing' process (or, as Jung conceived his kind of psychology, a "healing way"), but a transformative process. It can only be wisely used by men or women who have experienced at least a 'rite of passage' marking the entrance to 'the Path'. In the past this passage and implications were a jealousy guarded secret, and involved harsh tests of *personal* Initiation. The person, as a product of biology and culture, had to prove himself or herself able to surrender totally to a power essentially working from the outside. But once the individual status is reached and the principle of subjectivity operates at the center of an autonomous and self-actualized human being—as the individualized, subjective 'I'—the passage to a transindividual level can occur in a more internal, more conscious, and presumably less formalized manner. Life itself, and the complex interplay among individuals or individuals-in-the-making, each struggling to assert autonomy and uniqueness, become the Tester.

As always, the first test is overcoming the inertia of the past. From a transpersonal point of view, the birth-chart represents the stage on which the Great War, like the one described in the *Bhagavad Gita*, or in a different sense the alchemical Great Work, takes place. It also indicates the relative potential strengths of the factors involved in the

---

*Cf. in my book *Fire Out of the Stone*.

conflict or transmutation. But this is only the beginning.

In theory, the newborn's first *in-breathing* impresses the potential solution of the basic problems life will present upon his or her etheric body—but there is nothing yet in the body to be conscious of and to hold this primordial revelation. The first *out-breathing* (the 'first cry') represents the answer of the body to the revelation—an unconscious, strictly biological response. Then life-in-the-body begins, as heart, lungs, and nerves become definitely interconnected according to the fundamental rhythm of the *biological* selfhood. Eventually, a collective-socio-cultural personality develops through family contacts and education; then perhaps a truly individualized selfhood, at least relatively free from bondage to biology and culture, autonomous and self-actualizing.

If there is a step beyond individuality—if *fulfillment* of individual selfhood is not accepted as an end in itself, but rather as an illusory goal that must be deliberately discarded—then the dynamic intensity of the process of *transformation* increases. The birth-chart is now seen as an altar on which the fire of constant overcoming must burn. That fire can be watched by the transpersonal astrologer as he or she studies the progressions of the whole chart (and particularly of the Sun and the Moon), then the transits of the personal, social, and transformative planets. What counts is the dynamism of the process. Everything is seen moving, active, interacting—playing its role in the great drama of the transmutation of the 'I' into the 'We', of individual consciousness into Pleroma consciousness.

Thus a new astrology takes form—always challenging, never to be fully objectivated and solidified into the safe patterns of standardized meaning: transpersonal astrology, to be used only *by* individuals and *for* individuals in whom the fire of transformation burns.

This fire is a subtle power, relentless in its consistency. It flows up, in antiphony with the descent of spirit-manifesting light. It is a song that has forgotten the notes many cultures have produced during many individual lives. At times, this song may seem tragic, even ruthless, but it always is inherently peace. It is the song of the Sage within the heart—a song of love escaped from the prison of pain. In it, the Yang of spirit and the Yin of transhuman desire blend in a silence that is wisdom—that is nothing, yet embraces everything. It is the Whole singing Itself 'I' in a myriad of silences.

# INDEX

## A

Akasha, 112
Andrews, Donald Hatch, 37
Angles, of birth-chart, 157; progressed Moon crossing, 170. See also Horizon, Meridian, Ascendant, Descendant, Midheaven, Zenith, Nadir, I.C.
Anima, 88, 104, 110
Ascendant, 70, 81, 83, 157, 161; progressed Moon crossing, 170, 173. See also Horizon, Angles, Birth (moment of)
Aspects, 76, 119, 153; "waxing", 155; "waning", 155
Asteroids, 120
Astrologer, responsibility of, 119, 125
Astrologer-Client Relationship, 53, 115, 120, 194
Astrology, esoteric, 115; humanistic, 22, 115; learning through biographical studies, 54, 121; multilevel approach to, 31, 51, 190, 195; myth of, 36; orbital, 70; person-centered, 115, 117, 134, 150, 173, 190; purpose of, 24, 28; transpersonal, 22, 25, 41, 45, 97, 99, 113, 115, 121, 133, 134, 136, 150, 156, 161, 165, 173, 190, 191, 197, 198; Uranian, 115
Atman, 73, 139
Atomism, 20, 31
Aurobindo, Sri, 27, 102

## B

'Benefic', 68
Biological Level, 46, 51, 55-60, 63, 64, 68, 75, 82, 84, 86, 105, 107, 111, 112, 183; biological selfhood, 79, 198; planets at the (see individual planetary listings); zodiac at the, 86
Birth, moment of, 40, 137, 161, 181, 198

Birth-Chart, 40, 109, 114, 123, 126, 130, 133, 134, 149, 160, 161, 163, 174, 182, 183, 197; at sociocultural level, 65; at individual level, 86, 165; at transpersonal level, 126, 136, 165; center of, 76, 85, 109; circumference of, 85; 'good' or 'bad', 152; as mandala, 77, 81, 85, 109, 149; Uranus, Neptune and Pluto in, 73, 90
Blavatsky, H.P., 120
Brahmam, 78
Buddha, 35, 44, 141

## C

Causality, 128, 130. See also Karma
Character, 62, 86, 128
Christ, 16, 34
Collective Psychism, 61, 62, 87, 140. See also Psychism, Sociocultural level
Comets, 60
Complexes, psychological, 87, 177
Conditioning, 127
Conjunction, 153, 154
Cosmobiology, 115
Counterindividual Factor, 88, 104. See also Soul
Culture, 47, 60. See also Sociocultural level
Culture-Whole, 62, 66

## D

Day-Force, 18
Deconditioning, 44
Descendant, 70, 81; progressed Moon crossing, 171. See also Angles, Horizon
Dharma, 27, 84, 130, 131, 152, 157, 160, 161, 179, 189
Diamond Soul, 159
'Divine Marriage', 98, 113, 141 190

**E**

Eclipses, 60, 69, 88
Ego, 62, 63, 76, 77, 87, 96, 102
108, 180
Esoteric Astrology, 115
Events, 114, 178
Evolution, 97, 100, 103

**F**

Fact, 30, 34
Father (hood), 57, 63
Fixed Stars, 58, 60. See also
'Star'
Freud, S., 21; Freudian sub-
conscious, 91
Fulfillment vs. Transformation,
95, 113, 115, 116, 132, 150, 198

**G**

Galaxy, 84, 98, 105, 109, 139
145, 184
Galileo, 25
Gandhi, 16
Genius, 90, 132
Gestalt, 149
Goethe, 110, 120, 140
'growth,' personal, 116, 190. See
also Fulfillment vs. Transform-
ation

**H**

'Higher Collectivity', 107, 134,
137, 140, 145, 173, 180, 184.
See also Pleroma
Holarchy, 110, 130, 190, 196
Holism, 20, 31
Horizon, line of, 70, 81, 85, 150
160. See also Ascendant,
Descendant
Horizontal Relationship, 129,
190. See also Holarchy
Houses (astrological), 119, 146,
160, 175; lunar progressions
through, 171; at transpersonal
level, 146. See also Horizon,
Meridian, Ascendant, Descend-
ant, Midheaven, Zenith, Im-
mum Coeli, Nadir
Human Potential Movement, 22
Humanistic Astrology 22, 115.
See also Person-centered astro-
logy
Humanity, see Planetary Being

**I**

'I' (real 'I', principle of indi
vidual selfhood), 65, 77, 82, 85,
89, 95, 96, 107, 108, 109, 110,
111, 113, 134, 137, 143, 145,
156, 157, 160, 180, 197, 198
'I', sense of being, 64, 76, 81,
102, 103, 156, 190
I.C., 82, 83, 84. See also
Meridian, Nadir, Angles
'I-center', 82, 86, 87, 89, 91,
95, 96, 102, 105, 110, 111, 113,
116, 132, 142, 146, 149, 154,
158, 184, 196
I.C.H.A. (International Committee for a Humanistic Astrology),
ix
I Ching, 3
Identity, 64, 68, 76, 89, 173
Immum Coeli, see I.C.
Individual (individualized person), 48, 87, 90, 97, 101, 127;
level, 48, 72, 83, 84, 86, 103,
105, 118, 137, 165, 183; self-
hood at individual level, see 'I',
'I-center', Selfhood
Individualistic Level, 50, 94
Individualization, process of, 40
48, 50, 65, 73, 77, 79, 82, 84, 85,
88, 89, 96, 101, 107, 125, 137,
140, 181
Individuation, process of, 111
Information, 28, 38, 119
Intelligence, 168
Intuition, 55, 112

**J**

Jung, C.G., 21, 64, 81, 91, 104
109, 110, 111, 140, 189, 197
Jupiter, 94, 95, 154; at biological level, 58, 144; at sociocultural level, 67, 69, 89, 94,
144; at individual level, 89; at
transpersonal level, 144, 154;
transits of, 185

**K**

Kabbalah, 80
Karma, 27, 71, 118, 128, 130,
131, 141, 152, 160, 166, 179,
190
Knowledge, 6, 14, 28, 29, 34
Korzsybski, Count Alfred, 101

## L

Lao Tze, 16
Levels, 26, 28, 31, 42, 52, 83, 195; change from one level to another, 52, 92, 108; four levels of human functioning, 46-51
Lights, 57, 59, 69, 153
'Lower Collectivity', 134, 137, 140, 145, 173, 180
Lunar Eclipse, 70
Lunation Cycle, 153, 173

## M

'Malefic', 68
Man, 42, 80, 96
Mandala, 77, 81, 85, 87, 91, 97, 109, 111, 156, 158, 160; center of, 139
Mandala of personality, 77, 85, 87, 91, 102, 105, 109, 157, 158, 184; center of, 85, 91 111
Mars, 94, 95, 185; at biological level, 58, 143, 153; at sociocultural level, 67, 143; at individual level, 89, 143; at transpersonal level, 143, 145, 188
Maslow, Abraham, 22, 46
Matriarchy, 57
May, Rollo, 22
Meaning, 13, 17, 28, 29, 34, 42 119
Mental Level, 62
Mercury, at biological level, 59, 68; at sociocultural level, 69; at individual level, 88; at transpersonal level, 141, 142, 144; transits of, 184
Meridian, 70, 82, 85, 150, 160. See also Midheaven, Zenith, I.C., Nadir, Angles
'Middle Way', 44
Midheaven, 70, 82, 83, 84, 188; progressed Moon over, 171. See also Meridian, Angles, Zenith
Milky Way, 84, 98, 105, 109, 139, 160. See also Galaxy
Milner, Antony, 175, 176
Mind, 100-113, 160; development of, 62, 101, 137

Moon, 69, 88; at biological level, 57, 63; at sociocultural level, 63, 66, 67, 76, 78; at individual level, 87, 88; at transpersonal level, 139, 141, 173; progressed, 170
Moon's Nodes, 69
Mother(hood), 63, 74
Mother Mira, 27

## N

Nadir, 70, 82, 83, 84; progressed Moon over, 171. See also Meridian, I.C., Angles
Neptune, 60, 73, 91; at sociocultural level, 72; at individual level, 90, 91, 92, 94; at transpersonal level, 95, 144, 145, 146, 184; long sextile with Pluto, 155; penetration of orbit by Pluto, 148; transits of, 184, 187, 189
Neurosis, 62. See also Complexes, psychological
Newton, 25
Nietzsche, 37
Night-Force, 18
Nodes, 69-72; lunar, 69; planetary, 70, 71
North Node, 71

## O

One, 78, 103, 159
Opposition, 153
Orbital Astrology, 70

## P

Part of Fortune, 154
Pascal, 196
Patriarchy, 57
Person (at sociocultural level), 49, 60, 62, 68, 75, 107, 197. See also Sociocultural level
Person-Centered Astrology, 115, 117, 134, 150, 173, 190. See also Humanistic astrology
Persona, 64
Planetary Being (Humanity), 109 110, 130, 132, 145
Planetary Nodes, 70, 71

Planets, at biological level, 56; at sociocultural level, 63-68, 72-74; in process of individualization, 94; at individual level, 87, 88-94; at transpersonal level, 138-149; bipolar pairs of, 155. See also Sun, Moon, Mercury, Venus, Mars, Jupiter, Saturn, Uranus, Neptune, Pluto

Pleroma, 79, 102, 105, 107, 109 110, 111, 143, 184, 196, 198. See also 'Higher collectivity'

Pluto, 60, 73; at sociocultural level, 72; at individual level, 90, 93, 94; at transpersonal level, 95, 144, 145, 147, 184; long sextile with Neptune, 155; penetration of Neptune's orbit by, 148; transits of, 147, 184, 187, 189

Prana, 61

Progressions, 113, 114, 121, 123, 134, 161, 164, 180; progressed lunation cycle, 173-177; 180; progressed-to-natal, 174, 179; progressed-to-progressed, 174, 179; secondary, 166; solar arc, 167; symbolic nature of, 169, 181, 182; at transpersonal level, 178

Proserpine, 189

'Psychic', 87, 120

Psychism, 61, 62, 76, 168, 180. See also Collective psychism

Ptolemy, 21, 115

**Q**

Quickening, 40

**R**

Radix System, of progressions, 167

Reincarnation, 128, 132

Rogers, Carl, 22

Rulership, 59

**S**

Sage, the, 12, 141, 198

Sagesse, 12, 13

Saturn, 60, 91, 94, 95, 139, 154, 179; at biological level, 58, 144; at sociocultural level, 63, 67, 68, 69, 74, 76, 78, 94, 144; at individual level, 89; at transper-

sonal level, 144, 158; return, 186; transits of, 185

Secondary Progressions, 166. See also Progressions SELF. 78, 103, 159

'Self', 63, 78

Selfhood, principle of individual, 79, 107, 109

Semi-Square, 153

Sepharial, 167

Shadow, 140

Sign, 28, 34, 46

Smuts, Jan, 20

Sociocultural Level, 47, 60, 63 68, 75, 82, 83, 84, 86, 89, 90, 96, 105, 107, 108, 127, 183; ego at, 63, 76, 77; selfhood at, 79; zodiac at, 86

Solar Arc Progressions, 167. See also Progressions

Solar Eclipse, 69

'Solar Progressions', 166. See also Progressions

Soul, 88, 101, 104, 105, 106, 107, 108, 110, 111, 113, 137, 139, 154

South Node, 71

Spengler, 106

Spirit, 97, 100

Square, 153

'Star', 84, 84, 98, 105, 109, 111, 118, 159, 181, 184

Sun, 88, 179; at biological level, 57, 63, 138; at sociocultural level, 64, 66, 138; at individual level, 86, 138; at transpersonal level, 139, 141

Sun-Sign, 86, 164

Sutich, Anthony, 22

Symbol, 29, 34, 46, 50, 103, 161, 193

'Synchronicity', 182

Synthesis, 20, 38, 44

**T**

Talent, 90

Transformation, process of, 94, 116, 133, 134, 151, 188

Transits, 113-114, 121, 123, 134, 161, 164, 180-191; repetitive patterns of, 184; symbolic nature of, 182

Transindividual Being(s), 101, 112, 181; level, 197; power, 83; self, 111. *See also* 'Star'

Transpersonal, 27, 50, 99; path, 84, 98, 112, 131, 132, 177; process, 27, 94, 114

Transpersonal Astrologer, 117, 120

Transpersonal Astrology, 22, 25, 41, 45, 97, 99, 113, 115, 121, 133, 134, 136, 150, 156, 161, 165, 173, 190, 191, 197, 198

Transpersonal Individual, 112

Transpersonal Level, 50, 114, 183; astrology at, 114; *see also* Transpersonal astrology; birthchart at, 113, *see also* Birthchart, selfhood at, *see* 'Star', Pleroma, Transindividual being

**U**

Unconscious, the, 104

Understanding, 34

Uranian Astrology, 115

Uranus, 60, 68, 73; at sociocultural level, 72; at individual level, 90, 91, 92, 94; at transpersonal level, 95, 144, 145, 146, 153, 184; transits of, 184, 187, 189

**V**

Venus, 185; at biological level, 58, 142; at sociocultural level, 67, 142; at individual level, 89, 142; at transpersonal level, 142, 144; transits of, 184

Vertical Relationship, 130. *See also* Holarchy

Vitalism, Vitalistic Age, 21, 57

**W**

Will, 86, 88, 139, 158

**Y**

Yang, 3, 108, 140, 141, 199; way or approach, 4, 18, 28, 44, 106

Yin, 3, 108, 140, 141, 199; way or approach, 10, 22, 28, 44, 106

**Z**

Zenith, 82, 83, 84, 98, 110, 159. *See also* Meridian, Midheaven, Angles

Zodiac, 59, 65, 84, 86, 167; at biological level, 86; at sociocultural level, 86; at individual level, 86; lunar, 57; solar, 57